NAPOLEON'S SOLDIERS

The *Grande Armée* of 1807 as Depicted
in the Paintings of the Otto Manuscript

NAPOLEON'S SOLDIERS

The Grande Armée of 1807 as Depicted
in the Paintings of the Otto Manuscript

GUY C. DEMPSEY, JR.

ARMS AND
ARMOUR

This book is dedicated to
My Parents, My Sisters, Joan and Anne,
My wife, Nancy,
and Katie, Elizabeth and Laura

Arms and Armour Press
An Imprint of the Cassell Group
Wellington House 125 Strand, London WC2R oBB

Distributed in the USA by Sterling Publishing Co. Inc.,
387 Park Avenue South, New York, NY 10016-8810.

Distributed in Australia by Capricorn Link (Australia) Pty. Ltd,
2/13 Carrington Road, Castle Hill, NSW 2154.

First published in Great Britain in 1994
Reprinted 1995

British Library Cataloguing-in-Publication Data:
a catalogue record for this book is available from the
British Library

ISBN 1-85409-242-1

Designed and edited by DAG Publications Ltd.
Designed by David Gibbons; edited by Michael Boxall.

Printed & bound in Slovenia by Printing House DELO-Tiskarna
by arrangement with Korotan Ljubljana

CONTENTS

Acknowledgements, 8

Preface, 9

I   ANALYSIS OF THE MANUSCRIPT, 11

1. Dating of the Manuscript, 13

2. Reliability of the Manuscript, 17

II   THE PAINTINGS, 25

Part I The Imperial Guard, 25

1. Untitled [French Marshal], 30

2. Sapper of the Foot Grenadiers of the Guard, 32

3. Drummer of the Foot Guard, 34

4. Officer of the Foot Guard, 36

5. Foot Grenadiers of the Guard, 38

6. Sapper of the Chasseurs of the Foot Guard, 40

7. Foot Chasseurs of the Guard, 42

8. Fusilier [-Grenadier] of the Guard, 44

9. Naval Soldiers [of the Guard], 46

10. Trumpeter of the Mounted Grenadiers of the Guard, 48

11. Mounted Grenadier of the Guard [Front view], 50

12. Mounted Grenadier of the Guard [Back view], 52

13. Trumpeter of the Mounted Chasseurs of the Guard, 54

14. Mounted Chasseur of the Guard, 56

15. Mameluke, 58

16. Trumpeter of the Mounted Dragoons of the Guard, 60

17. Mounted Dragoon of the Guard, 62

18. Office of [Guard] Horse Artillery, 64

19. [Guard] Horse Artillery, 66

20. Elite [Orderly] Gendarme [of the Guard], 68

21. Mounted Grenadier [Guides of the Prince of Neufchâtel], 70

Part II. Line Infantry, 73

22. Sapper of the 3rd Regiment, 78

23. Officer and Grenadier of the 3rd Regiment, 80

24. Officer and Voltigeur of the 3rd Regiment, 82

25. Drum Major of the 8th Regiment, 84

26. Sapper of the 8th Regiment, 86

27. Office rand Grenadier of the 8th Regiment, 88

28. Officer of Voltigeurs of the 8th Regiment, 90

29. [Voltigeur and Fusilier of the] 8th Regiment, 92

30. Officer and Fusilier of the 8th Regiment, 94

31. Sapper of the 21st Regiment, 96

32. Officer and Grenadier of the 21st Regiment, 98

33. Officer and Voltigeur of the 21st Regiment, 100

34. Office rand Fusilier of the 21st Regiment, 102

35. Sapper of the 22nd Regiment, 104

36. Officer and Grenadier of the 22nd Regiment, 106

37. Officer and Voltigeur of the 22nd Regiment, 108

38. Sapper of the 24th Regiment, 110

39. Officer and Grenadier of the 24th Regiment, 112

40. Officer and Voltigeur of the 24th Regiment, 114

41. Sapper of the 25th Regiment, 116

42. Sapper of the 45th Regiment, 118

43. Grenadier and Drum Major of the 45th Regiment, 120

44. Sapper of the 46th Regiment, 122

45. Officer and Voltigeur of the 46th Regiment, 124

46. Sapper of the 63rd Regiment, 126

47. Sapper of the 63rd Regiment, 128

48. Officer and Grenadier of the 63rd Regiment, 130

49. Drum Major of the 75th Regiment, 132

50. Sapper of 85th Regiment, 134

51. Officer and Grenadier of the 85th Regiment, 136

52. Officer and Voltigeur of the 85th Regiment, 138

53. Sapper of the 94th Regiment, 140

54. Grenadier and Voltigeur of the 94th Regiment, 142

55. Sapper of the 95th Regiment, 144

56. Officer and Grenadier of the 95th Regiment, 146

57. Sapper of the 96th Regiment, 148

58. Drum Major of the 96th Regiment, 150

59. [Grenadier and Fusilier of the] 96th Regiment, 152

60. Officer and Voltigeur of the 96th Regiment, 154

Part III. Light Infantry and Non-Line Troops, 157

61. Grenadier [Carabinier] Officer of the 9th Regiment of Foot chasseurs [Light Infantry], 162

62. Grenadier and Fusilier [Carabinier and Chasseur] of the 9th Regiment of Foot chasseurs [Light Infantry], 164

63. Sapper of the 10th Regiment of Foot Chasseurs [Light Infantry], 166

64. Sapper of the 16th Regiment [of] Chasseurs [Light Infantry], 168

65. Drum Major of the 16th Regiment of Foot Chasseurs [Light Infantry], 170

66. Grenadier [Carabinier] and Chasseur [Voltigeur] of the 16th Regiment [of Light Infantry], 172

67. Drum Major and Chasseur of the Guard of Paris, 174

68. Officer and Grenadier of the Guard of Paris, 176

Part IV. Line Cavalry, 179

69. Cuirassier [Mounted Carabinier], 184

70. Cuirassier, 186

71. Cuirassier of the 9th Regiment, 188

72. Trumpeter of the 9th Regiment of Cuirassiers, 190
73. Officer of the 3rd Regiment of Dragoons, 192
74. Dragoon of the 3rd Regiment, 194
75. Mounted Sapper of the 11th (?) Regiment of Dragoons, 196
76. Dragoons of the 20th (?) and 6th (?) Regiments, 198
77. Hussar [Chasseur] of the 5th Regiment, 200
78. Grenadier [Elite Trooper] of the 24th Regiment of Mounted Chasseurs, 202
79. Trumpeter of the 24th Regiment of Mounted Chasseurs, 204
80. Officer of the 24th Regiment of Mounted Chasseurs, 206
81. [Trooper of the] 24th Regiment of Mounted Chasseurs, 208
82. Grenadier [Elite Trooper] of the 26th Regiment of Mounted Chasseurs, 210
83. Hussar of the 2nd Regiment, 212
84. Grenadier [Elite Trooper of the 5th Regiment] of Hussars, 214
85. Grenadier [Elite Trooper of the 7th (?) Regiment] of Hussar, 216

Part V. Artillery and Support Troops, 219
86. Horse Artillery, 222
87. Foot Artillery [1st Battalion of Sappers], 224
88. Soldier and Officer of the Artillery Train, 226
89. Gendarme, 228

Part VI. Italian Troops, 231
90. Sapper of the 1st Italian [Line] Regiment, 234
91. Officer and Grenadier of the 1st Italian Line Regiment, 236
92. Office rand Voltigeur of the First Italian [Line] Regiment, 238
93. Chasseur and Grenadier [Carabinier] of the 1st Regiment of Italian Chasseurs [Light Infantry], 240
94. Chasseur [Voltigeur] of the 1st Regiment of Italian Chasseurs [Light Infantry] and Grenadier [Carabinier of the 2nd Light], 242
95. Sapper of the First Regiment of Italian Chasseurs [Light Infantry], 244
96. Drum Major of the First Regiment of Italian Chasseurs [Light Infantry], 246
97. Chasseur [Voltigeur] of 1st Italian [Line] Regiment; Grenadier [Carabinier] of 2nd Regiment of Italian Chasseurs [Light Infantry], 248
98. Italian Artilleryman [Sapper]; Grenadier [Carabinier] of the Third [Second] Regiment of Italian Chasseurs [Light Infantry], 250

Appendixes, 253

Appendix A. List of Units Depicted in the Otto Manuscript (by type), 254

Appendix B. Organization of the Grand Army, 1 June, 1807, 255

ACKNOWLEDGEMENTS

This book represents the first book-length product of a lifelong interest in Napoleonic military history and uniforms, and so when I think of people to acknowledge for their assistance in its creation, I am compelled to mention first the members of my family, who have always tolerated (and sometimes even encouraged) my idiosyncratic pursuits. In terms of this particular volume, my greatest debt is owed to my wife, Nancy, who has never begrudged me the time necessary for its completion, but Katie and Elizabeth also deserve credit for sharing their computer and playroom with me. Laura contributed in her own important way by not arriving until after the manuscript was finished.

Next in priority are the friends and acquaintances who have corresponded with me over the years on topics of mutual interest and who have been extraordinarily generous in sharing advice and substantive information: Colonel John Elting. George Nafziger, Peter Hofschröer, Piero Crociani, J.-P. Loriot, Markus Gärtner, Friedrich Herrman and G. Flotté. In addition to Napoleonic expertise, all these men share a common respect for primary sources and careful historical method. I would also like to remember in this regard the late Andrew Zaremba and his kindness in passing on much knowledge and wisdom which is not found in printed works. In writing this book I have tried to be faithful to his uncompromising research standards. I also need to acknowledge a debt to the trio of Frenchmen who have done most to advance the modern study of Napoleonic military uniforms: the late Lucien Rousselot, Albert Rigondaud and Michel Pétard. Although I have on occasion found it necessary to question some of their conclusions, this work would not have been possible without the foundation laid by these men.

Special thanks for this book are due to Peter Harrington, the curator of The Anne S. K. Brown Military Collection. His co-operation, which was obviously vital to the completion of the project, was given freely and enthusiastically on all occasions.

PREFACE

The Anne S. K. Brown Military Collection is one of only a handful of collections in the world devoted to military iconography.[1] As such, it is a repository of literally thousands of books, prints and pieces of original artwork about military dress throughout history, and amidst such an abundance of material there are plenty of rare gems of information to be found.

One such item is the bound set of gouache (opaque watercolour) paintings of Napoleonic soldiers which can be found in the Collection under the unpretentious title of 'Set of 98 Contemporary Watercolours'. This is without doubt the very same set that is known in most Napoleonic circles by the name of the 'Otto Manuscript', so called because it is said that it was once the property of a certain Major Otto of Baden.[2] It is also without doubt one of the premier original sources available today for the study of Napoleonic military uniforms.

The Otto paintings first came to modern notice when they were acquired earlier in this century by M. Albert Depreaux, a prominent member of 'La Sabretache', the famous association of French experts and amateurs interested in military history and uniforms. During the Second World War, several hand-coloured sets of facsimiles of the paintings owned by M. Depreaux were made by Lucien Rousselot, the renowned French military artist.[3] It is through these copies (and second and third generations of these copies) that the paintings have become best known to modern students of Napoleonic uniformology.[4] The originals were sold after the war to Mrs Brown, which is why they now repose in the collection bearing her name at Brown University in Providence, Rhode Island.

These beautiful paintings deserve to be brought to the attention of a wider audience on aesthetic grounds alone, but the focus of this volume is more on their historical significance than on their indisputably decorative qualities. The Otto Manuscript is, very simply, a unique window on history that brings Napoleonic soldiers and uniforms into view in a way that is almost unprecedented for a pre-photographic era. These paintings are not stylized prints or lifeless salon artwork created long after the event. They are a precise, vibrant record of an amateur artist's first-hand observations, imbued with a spectacular intimacy as a result of his talent for faithfully reproducing even small details of dress and equipment.

The bulk of this book consists of reproductions of the Otto paintings accompanied by individual commentaries identifying points of interest and comparing and contrasting the uniform information presented with that available from other sources. Before we turn to the paintings themselves, however, it is important to take a critical look at the Manuscript so as to determine whether it is worthy of being treated as a unique primary source of research information.

1   For the background to the Collection, see the anecdotal story of Mrs. Brown's interest in military uniforms detailed in Susan Hack, 'A Love Affair with Uniforms', *MHQ: The Quarterly Journal of Military History* Vol. 1, No. 2 (Winter 1989), pp. 98–109.

2   R. D. Stiot, 'Sur la Suite du Major Otto', *Carnet de la Sabretache* N.S. No. 27 (2nd Trimester 1975), p. 47 (hereinafter referred to as 'Stiot's Article').

3   Rousselot (1900–1992) was the creator of a series of over 100 uniform plates with text entitled *L'Armée Française – Ses Uniformes, Son Armament, Son Equipement* (hereinafter, the 'Rousselot Plates') which is perhaps the most important modern compilation of information on the uniforms of Napoleon's armies, even though it lacks a systematic citation of sources.

4   For instance, the author of this work owns a set of modern black and white facsimiles of the Otto paintings produced by M. Henri Achard, a French gentleman who has devoted many years to creating reproductions of important Napoleonic uniform sources.

I

ANALYSIS OF
THE MANUSCRIPT

I
ANALYSIS OF
THE MANUSCRIPT

The serious study of military uniforms of the Napoleonic era is such a narrow field of scholarly endeavour that it is difficult at times to remember that it is still part of the broad discipline of historical research. Such study must consequently be based on reliable, first-hand information if it is to produce trustworthy and useful results. Unfortunately, much modern work on Napoleonic uniforms is based solely on information derived from secondary sources which lack the requisite measure of reliability. Moreover, even when information from primary sources has been presented, it is rarely subjected to critical review and its value is often further diminished by a lack of specific citations of the sources used.

The Otto Manuscript, on the other hand, appears on its face to be a primary source that presents a detailed and visually striking portrait of an enormous array of Napoleonic uniforms and thus appears to be an exceptional resource for learning more about military dress of that era. Of course, the problem arises with the word 'appears'; the Otto Manuscript is only of interest in this regard if that appearance is borne out by substance. The Manuscript must consequently be tested to see if it has both the essential characteristics that distinguish primary from secondary sources. If the paintings are (1) authentically contemporary to the Napoleonic period and (2) the product of eye-witness observation of the clothing they depict, they are entitled to a unique place in the iconography of military dress of the First Empire because no other original pictorial source has detailed captions that explicitly connect specific uniforms with specific French military formations. If they lack one or both of these characteristics, the value of the paintings as a research tool is correspondingly diminished. The conclusion of this study is that the Manuscript possesses both these characteristics to a significant degree. First, there is very strong circumstantial evidence that the Manuscript is contemporary to the Napoleonic era and, indeed, that the paintings can be reasonably dated to the year 1807. Secondly, the depictions of military costumes in the Otto Manuscript contain so many details that can be verified by reference to other established primary sources that the most reasonable explanation for the extent of the coincidence is that the paintings must be an authentic record of soldiers and uniforms actually seen by the Otto artist.

1. Dating of the Manuscript

With iconographic material such as the Otto Manuscript the two usual (and easiest) ways to determine whether a work is contemporary to a particular period are (1) to find a date on the work itself or (2) identify the artist involved, but neither of these approaches is workable in this case. Although the uniforms depicted are unmistakably French (for the most part) and unmistakably Napoleonic, the paintings themselves are most definitely undated. Clearly, they cannot have been created later than the date in this century when the Manuscript was 'discovered' by M. Depreaux, but establishing more positive information about the age of the Manuscript beyond that point is a difficult proposition.[1] As for dating it by reference to the artist responsible, the consistency of style and materials used in the paintings makes inescapable the conclusion that the Otto Manuscript is the work of a single artist, but there is no intrinsic evidence of his identity such as a signature or initials. The artist consequently remains anonymous notwithstanding one serious recurring suggestion that the Otto paintings are the work of an early nineteenth-century German artist named Kolb or Kolbe.

The origin of the artistic attribution of the Manuscript to Kolb is unknown, but according to Stiot's Article it is based on 'undeniable similarities' between the Otto figures and those in two large prints, one depicting French Imperial Guard cavalry and the other mounted troops of the Russian Imperial Guard, which are said to be the work of an artist named 'Kolb'. Unhappily for the purposes of verifying this story, neither of these prints can be traced today.[2] Both Lucien Rousselot and Albert Rigondaud (better known as 'Rigo')[3] apparently accept this attribution and make reference to paintings by 'Kolb' and 'Kolbe' in their respective works.[4] Nevertheless, neither of these experts has ever publicly set forth an independent justification for his position. Indeed, Rousselot's statements on the subject have at times been less than decisive: 'Although the origin of these water-colours is uncertain, some informed amateurs and expert connoisseurs of the iconography of the imperial epoch have attributed them to the German artist Kolbe. That is possible, but the paintings might also be the work of an unknown Frenchman.'[5] Rigo is more decisive and (citing information received from Jean

Brunon) has stated in correspondence with the author of this volume that the artist can, in fact, be specifically identified as Carl Wilhelm Kolbe 'the Younger' (1781–1853). A standard reference work provides the information that Kolbe was a prize-winning painter of historical subjects (albeit generally of a classical nature) and that he even did a painting of the Battle of the Katzbach, but there is no mention of any works similar to these uniform studies.[6]

The Kolbe attribution therefore seems to be the product of collective assertion rather than concrete evidence. It also seems contrary to common sense, since the Otto artist's mastery of detail and colour cannot conceal his limited command of other techniques which would be routine for any professional painter. The paintings are all carefully finished works rather than careless sketches, and yet most have decidedly unprofessional defects of depth and perspective and the poses used are stylized and repetitive. The paintings also have only the most rudimentary of backgrounds. It therefore seems more reasonable to conclude that the Otto artist was an anonymous amateur, which is the conclusion reached by M. Depreaux himself and with which Mrs Brown concurred.[7]

Some few deductions can be made about the identity of this unknown artist, but unfortunately none of them helps materially in establishing the date of the work. For instance, given the choice of subject matter for the paintings and the clarity of the details illustrated, the artist was apparently a person both familiar with and interested in military uniforms, perhaps as a result of prior military service. The artist was therefore also more likely to have been a man rather than a woman. Further, the fact that all the captions, which appear to be the same age as the paintings and are therefore likely to have been written by the artist himself, are in the French language provides straightforward evidence for a conclusion that the artist was a Frenchman. (The purpose, date and creator of the marginal pencil paintings and notations which appear on some of the plates cannot be as clearly ascertained on the evidence available.) The mistakes in the captions, which are particularly glaring in respect of the cavalry figures, strongly suggest that the artist was not familiar with mounted troops.

In some cases where the artist is unknown, the provenance of a work can supply the missing link to the desired time period by providing a chain of ownership running back to the date of the work's creation. Here again, however, the easy solution has been lost because nothing is known of the history of the Manuscript prior to its appearance in Germany earlier in this century. The Manuscript apparently originally included other paintings in addition to those purchased by M. Depreaux,[8] but the disposition of these other paintings is not recorded and their whereabouts is unknown, so any information they might provide about the origins of the Manuscript is unavailable. The same artist may also have created other similar works which could be traced independently, but investigation of the one promising case known to the author yields only disappointing results.

That case involves a gouache painting of figures of the French Imperial Guard which is painted in a style that is almost identical (down to the very poses of the figures) to that of the Otto paintings, although the composition is quite different since it contains six figures, three in the foreground and three in the background.[9] When this work, which is in the Beunon Collection of the French Army Museum, was used in 1955 as a black-and-white illustration for a book on the Imperial Guard, it was simply identified as 'a German gouache of the period', but by 1965 it had become catalogued as '*Officier et Grenadiers à pied de la Garde Impériale en surtout. Gouache par Wilhelm-Carl Kolbe*'.[10] This painting has also been reproduced in colour in a recent article about Guard Grenadier bearskin caps, this time with a caption which specifically asserts (without supporting evidence) that the work is part of the Otto Manuscript.[11] Unfortunately, repeated attempts to obtain further information about this painting directly from the Brunon Collection have been unsuccessful.

The next possibility for dating a pictorial work (other than scientific testing, which has not been possible in this case) is to look for evidence of age in the physical attributes of the work itself. This is the first approach that yields positive results for the Otto Manuscript because there are a number of aspects of the paintings that strongly suggest that they are indeed contemporary with the period of the uniforms depicted. Starting with the basics, both the paper and the paint used are consistent with the conclusion that the Manuscript was created during the Napoleonic era. The yellowed paper has a heavy fibre content and a regular pattern of linear markings, both of which features are visible to the naked eye against the light and can be found in much European paper made in the early nineteenth century. The paper also suffers to a slight degree from foxing, another (but less significant) indicator of age. The water-based gouache colours used in the paintings have for the most part remained almost suspiciously vivid, but there are other similar paintings from the First Empire such as the uniform studies of Nicolas Hoffman in the Bibliothèque Nationale in Paris which are equally well preserved.[12] In a few instances (as, for example, Plate No. 27 [Officer and Grenadier of the 8th Line]) the white pigment in a painting has suffered significant discoloration. This type of problem is identical with that which can be found affecting the white paint in many hand-coloured plates produced commercially during the Napoleonic period such as those in the well-known Martinet series.[13]

The watermarks in the paper for ten of the paintings provide even more clues to dating the paintings. None of them is complete, a circumstance which suggests that the paper used for the paintings was cut down from larger sheets, but the partial marks that are visible suggest very old paper of German origin. For instance, the watermark on Plate No. 41 (Sapper of the 25th Regiment) consists of the upper half of a medallion bearing the profile of a male figure, his hair tied back in a decidedly eighteenth-century queue secured by a bow, while that on Plate No. 44 (Sapper of the 46th Regiment) consists of the bottom of a medallion and the partial legend 'Fr. W II H II' (perhaps a reference to Frederick William II of Prussia, who died in 1797). The German connection is made more explicit by the appearance of the name 'F. W. MESCHMAN' in the watermark on Plate No. 49 (Drum Major of the 75th Regiment) and of the partial words or name 'SPECHT HAUSEN' in the paper for Plate No. 52 (Officer and Voltigeur of the 85th Regiment).

Certain features of the captions handwritten in ink on the paintings further support the conclusion that they are authentically contemporary. Both the style of penmanship and the faded brown colour of the ink are consistent with the appearance of the writing on other documents which can be indisputably dated to the Napoleonic period, as is the orthography of the captions themselves. For instance, the French word '*Sapeur*' appears in its archaic form spelled with two 'p's, while the second 's' in the words '*Chasseur*' and '*Cuirassier*' is written as an 'f' in accordance with the convention prevailing at the end of the eighteenth and beginning of the nineteenth centuries. The

word '*pied*' is also spelled in archaic fashion without the final 'd'.

Other significant information for dating of the Manuscript can be found in the identity of the units and uniforms that are the subjects of the paintings. (See Appendix A for a complete list of the units that appear in the Manuscript.) Unless the Otto artist imagined the soldiers he painted, he must have been working from direct observation because he has depicted many uniforms that are not illustrated in any other manuscript or printed sources. Given that reality, at least one painting can be dated with some confidence because it depicts a unit which, conveniently, was only in existence for a short period of time. Plate No. 20 (Elite [Orderly] Gendarme [of the Guard]) could not have been created before October 1806, the month in which the Gendarme Orderlies were formed, nor is it likely to have been painted much later than July 1807, the month in which this aristocratic formation was formally disbanded.[14] Similar chronological reference points are also available for other plates because of the history of the unit shown. For instance, the figure in Plate No. 8 (Fusilier [Grenadier] of the Guard) cannot have been observed and painted before that regiment was created in December of 1806.[15]

The styles and colours of the uniforms shown in the Manuscript also have chronological implications. The French Imperial Guard was known for its elegant full dress uniforms, but it is well-established that for the 1806–7 campaign these were replaced by simpler campaign uniforms of the type illustrated in the Manuscript. More significantly, the Manuscript depicts several figures in white uniforms, an atypical costume for French Napoleonic infantry worn only during a short period commencing in 1806 and officially ending in 1807, although many units would have continued to wear coats of that colour until stocks were exhausted.[16] Finally, the Voltigeur in Plate No. 24 (Officer and Voltigeur of the 3rd Regiment) cannot have been observed and painted very much later than 22 February 1808 because the base of the shako plate is depicted as being worn over the lower band of the shako, a placement that was prohibited by Colonel Laurent Schobert of the 3rd Regiment on that date.[17]

What emerges from all this information is the probability that the Otto Manuscript was created in its totality sometime in the period from September 1806 when the French Imperial Guard set off for Prussia wearing its undress uniforms, and the summer of 1808 when that part of the Grand Army that had not already returned to France was recalled from Germany to take part in Napoleon's Spanish campaign. This dating can perhaps be further refined by a comparison of the list of the units illustrated in the Otto paintings with orders of battle of the Grand Army. The earliest time when all the relevant formations were serving in the same theatre of war was the late spring and summer of 1807 when they were all attached to the Grand Army in northern Germany and Poland. (See Appendix B for an organizational chart of Napoleon's forces at that time.) This coincidence leads one to conclude that the Manuscript was created during the summer of 1807 after the Peace of Tilsit had been ratified and most active campaigning had come to an end.

2. Reliability of the Manuscript

A primary source is, in an historical sense, any body of material that is likely to provide a researcher with first-hand information about the subject under study. A source therefore cannot be considered primary unless it is contemporary with the relevant period, but the mere fact that a source is found to be contemporary does not alone entitle it to primary status. The other, equally essential prerequisite is that the source must be the product of direct contact between its creator and the subjects covered. This contact ensures that the information conveyed by the source has been filtered through only one layer of interpretation and therefore can still be reliably accurate. If other layers are involved, the source can only be secondary because the more layers there are, the more difficult it becomes to obtain a clear view of the original subject, even if the distortion from each layer is relatively slight. Consider, for instance, the hypothetical case of a painting of a French soldier created in 1807 by an American artist who had never travelled to Europe but who had spoken to veterans of the Grand Army. Such a painting would certainly be contemporary with the Napoleonic era and, depending on the descriptive powers of the veterans, it might even be accurate in many regards. It would not, however, be a primary source of information about French Napoleonic military dress; it would simply be a very old secondary source.

These observations on the nature of a primary source have one obvious implication for this study of the Otto Manuscript. Even if, on the basis of the evidence discussed above, its paintings can be considered to be authentically contemporary with the Napoleonic era, the Otto Manuscript cannot be accepted as reliable until it has been subjected to still another level of critical scrutiny. The purpose of this additional scrutiny is to determine whether it is reasonable to believe that the Otto artist actually observed the uniforms he painted and that therefore the Manuscript truly qualifies as a primary research source. In some cases, the necessary connection between an artist and his subjects is easy to establish because the artist has left a journal or memoir which tells where he travelled and what he saw.[18] In most cases (including this one), however, the record is silent. In the absence of such information, we must first consider if the paintings themselves tell us anything about why and how they were created that can shed light on the Manuscript's reliability. Next, and more importantly, we must analyse the reliability of the paintings by comparing the information about Napoleonic uniforms presented by the Manuscript with that derived from other established primary sources. While the results of the first stage of this scrutiny are inconclusive, those of the second stage definitively establish the Manuscript as a significantly reliable primary source.

The first, and most obvious, point that can be made about the Otto paintings in regard to their reliability is that they were apparently created for the express purpose of illustrating the military uniforms shown. The works are certainly not individual portraits, nor are they battle or even camp scenes; the focal points of each composition are the figures themselves. Moreover, although there is no evidence that the artist was working to a particular scale (in the scientific sense of that word), he certainly chose a size for the paintings that allows even small details to be visible.

This focus, particularly when accompanied by a systematic effort to record uniforms of different ranks in different units and to label them correctly, suggests some serious purpose, albeit one that may be impossible to identify from the distance of nearly 200 years. Perhaps the Otto artist was like Canon Antonio Rovatti (1763–1818), the Italian cleric who created an illustrated chronicle recording all the troops stationed in or passing through the City of Modena during the Revolutionary and Napoleonic eras.[19] Or he may have been like Andreas Ornstrup, a Danish artist who made paintings of the French and Spanish troops stationed in Denmark in 1807-8 in the hope of turning them into a series of prints that could be profitably sold to the public.[20] In either case, however, the motivation would have been consistent with direct contact between the artist and his subjects and with a desire on his part to make the paintings as accurate as possible.

No matter what deductions one makes about the artist's reasons for creating the paintings, his choice of specific units, and ranks within those units, for illustration in the Manuscript seems mysterious. If the Otto artist selected his subjects solely on the basis of geographic proximity and access, there would presumably not be so many cases of only one regiment in a brigade or division being singled out for inclusion. As to the breadth of coverage within particular units, some regiments such as the 8th Line Infantry and the 24th Chasseurs have a wide range of ranks and functions depicted. More commonly, however, one or more basic types are missing, and, invariably, there are no drummers or other musicians to go with the Drum Majors, all of which circumstances suggest that originally there may have been yet more paintings of French subjects in the collection and that these are now 'lost'. Leaving aside that tantalizing possibility, one searches in vain for a definitive common theme linking the units and ranks depicted.

One other intrinsic aspect of the paintings that is relevant to an analysis of the reliability of the Manuscript is the talent of the artist for clear and precise expression of detail, even while he was struggling on occasion with problems of perspective. The images are so well-defined that they inspire confidence that the paintings accurately reflect the uniforms viewed by the artist. This point, of course, is not, in and of itself, particularly persuasive because the artist could have been copying from other sources, but it becomes more so given the smattering of spectacularly obvious errors that characterize the work. These errors, such as misshapen and incomplete bridles and saddlery, could hardly have been made by a copyist. They are explainable, however, if one considers the possibility that the Otto artist was working from life. Since it is unlikely that French soldiers would have been willing to pose conveniently for extended periods, the Otto artist may have been obliged to create the paintings in two stages, first making sketches and notes as he observed his subjects and later converting these preliminary materials to finished paintings. This two-step process, with its built-in lag between observation and execution, could easily account for such defects because there would have been no opportunity to verify the completed work against the original model.

Since the paintings themselves provide only limited clues about their reliability, we must move on to the second stage of scrutiny to determine the decisive factors for establishing whether the Manuscript is truly reliable. These are both the extent to which, and the way in which, the uniform information provided by the Otto paintings can be corroborated with information available from other established primary sources for the study of Napoleonic military costume. The extent of corroboration (discussed at length below) is, in a word, impressive, but perhaps more important is the pattern of inter-relationship between the Manuscript and other sources.

If the uniforms in the Otto paintings were very similar to those depicted in only one other contemporary pictorial source or described in only one other written source, the Manuscript would have to be viewed with suspicion because there would be no way to negate the possibility that the paintings were actually based on those other sources and not on independent observation of the relevant uniforms. The information from the Manu-

script, however, is not highly correlated with that from any other single source; instead, it consists of a myriad of details most of which can only be corroborated by reference to information from a wide variety of sources, many of which are themselves relatively scarce or little-known. It is highly unlikely that a single artist, particularly a contemporary one (since some of the relevant sources did not become publicly available until long after the Napoleonic era had ended), could have been aware of enough of these sources to produce all the paintings in the Manuscript without having seen the subjects he was painting. The more reasonable conclusion is that the variety and diversity of corroboration derives from the fact that the Otto artist and the creators of the other sources were all recording first-hand information about the same military subjects.

Two examples from among the many available should suffice to demonstrate this point. The left-hand figure in Plate No. 29 ([Voltigeur and Fusilier of the] 8th Regiment) has a shako plate of unique shape, the central eagle design being stamped in the metal (as opposed to being cut out). Moreover, the crowned eagle is facing atypically to the right of the wearer and is placed over the abbreviated name of the regiment. All in all, this item of equipment is completely inexplicable, until, of course, one learns that there is a surviving example of an 8th Regiment shako plate in the Brunon Collection of the French Army Museum which is identical with that depicted by the Otto artist.[21] In Plate No. 48 (Officer and Grenadier of the 63rd Regiment) the collar and coloured piping of the officer's jacket surprisingly appear more orange than scarlet red, the colour one would expect to find used for those details. However, the recollections of an officer who joined the regiment in the summer of 1807 just happen to record: 'The 63rd was a disciplined... and well-dressed regiment. As an affectation, the colonel [Mouton-Duvernet] had adopted for the officers the distinctive colour (*aurore* [light orange] collar and piping) which the regiment was supposed to wear with the white uniform.'[22] There can be no doubt on the basis of such evidence that the Otto paintings are the accurate product of direct observation by the artist of the uniforms depicted.

The acceptance of the Otto Manuscript as a reliable primary source poses one special problem – that of evaluating the uniform details (and, in some cases, complete uniforms) which appear in the Manuscript but which are *not* confirmed by other sources. In such cases, the demonstrated reliability of the Manuscript must temper the scepticism which would normally be brought to bear on such details so that the unique information is treated as authentic until proven otherwise, no matter how many other sources contain contrary material. Precisely the greatest value of a source such as the Otto Manuscript is that it provides a foundation for re-appraisal of accepted wisdom and a catalyst for research in new directions. In particular, no detail of an Otto painting should be dismissed as a mistake of the artist without careful consideration (although common sense dictates that this consideration can occasionally be quite brief, as in a case where one cuff flap has buttons, but the other has none).

The process of corroborating the reliability of the Otto Manuscript by reference to other primary sources requires some appreciation of exactly what those other sources might be. The list below (which is arranged in accordance with the author's personal opinions concerning relative reliability) sets forth the basic categories of contemporary materials that have been used as sources for corroboration of the Manuscript's information about Napoleonic military uniforms and suggests the

different factors that can affect the reliability of such sources:

1. Sketches and paintings from life by professional artists. This type of iconographic source combines the accuracy of first-hand observation with the technical prowess of the trained artist and provides the greatest degree of reliability in the period before photography because the works are executed closer to the moment of observation than more formal studio pieces. *Examples:* Sketchbooks of Albrecht Adam.[23] *Critical Concerns:* Difficulty in establishing where and when a particular sketch was made; lesser degree of reliability when troops foreign to the home country of the artist are depicted.

2. Sketches and paintings from life by amateur artists. Similar reliability to Source No. 1, but style tends to be unpolished or naïve. *Examples:* The Otto Manuscript itself; the Manuscript of the 'Bourgeois' of Hamburg,[24] which depicts the troops of all nations that passed through Hamburg during the Napoleonic Wars; the Zimmerman drawings, which record the passage of troops through Berlin.[25] *Critical Concerns:* Lack of technical skill can lead to grotesque renderings of points of detail; the provenance of most manuscripts is scanty and many are known only through later copies of the work which have been intentionally or unintentionally altered or modified.

3. Formal paintings and other works (excluding portraits) by professional artists. This type of iconographic source includes the large commissioned battle paintings displayed at the salons of the period, which are somewhat stylized artistically but which had to be accurate enough to satisfy the critical eye of actual participants in the actions represented. *Examples:* Paintings by Louis-François Lejeune (1775–1848), Horace Vernet (1789–1863), Antoine-Jean Gros (1771–1835) and Charles Thevenin (1764–1838).

Critical Concerns: Time lapse between the incidents depicted and the execution of the work gives rise to anachronisms (e.g., Thevenin's painting at Versailles of the 1805 surrender of Ulm depicts figures from the Guard Dragoons and the Guard Polish Lancers, neither of which units existed in that year, but did exist when the picture was painted).

4. *Surviving items of clothing and equipment.* Artefacts provide the only true means of establishing exactly how a uniform looked and are the invaluable adjunct to the iconographic sources noted above.

Examples: Museum exhibitions; weapons and militaria sold by dealers.

Critical concerns: Many surviving items have been mis-identified or modified (e.g., by the addition of new lace or buttons) in the course of time, so the most reliable pieces are those that can be identified with a particular owner or incident (i.e., the uniform coat said to have been worn by a specific officer at Waterloo is likely to be more authentic than an anonymous officer's jacket); items may also become unintentionally altered as is the case with the numerous dragoon uniform jackets in the French Army Museum in Paris which are presently bright blue in colour because of the instability of green dye over time; outright forgeries have been known to occur.

5. *Official correspondence, inspection reports and inventories of clothing.* These written sources (as opposed to official regulations discussed below) complement the visual sources because they document the actual use of particular items of military dress at specific points in time. A report that the regimental shakos are in disrepair may not provide a clue as to the design of the headgear, but it does prove that shakos were worn.

Examples: Published correspondence of major figures such as Napoleon;[26] published collections of general orders; administrative papers in regimental and army archives.

Critical Concerns: Terminology is not used consistently so that a reference to *bonnets à poil* [fur bonnets] may mean different things in different sources.

6. *Private correspondence and diaries.* These sources provide a means of verifying the extent to which official regulations are actually given effect by or with respect to the troops concerned (e.g., a letter from a recruit stating that he was sent into battle with no uniform other than a greatcoat suggests possible breakdowns in supply and distribution arrangements). Sometimes individual soldiers include sketches of themselves in uniform in letters, thereby combining elements of Source No. 2 above as well.

Examples: The letters collected in E. Fairon and H. Heuse, *Lettres des Grognards* (Liège, 1936).

Critical Concerns: Inconsistent terminology; inability of the authors to express themselves clearly.

7. *Portraits (including miniatures).* This is the only source that captures the appearance of individual members of the armed forces.

Examples: The famous portrait of Lieutenant Dieudonné of the Imperial Guard Mounted Chasseurs by Jean-Louis André Théodore Géricault (1791–1824) which won the gold medal at the Salon of 1812 and which now hangs in the Louvre Museum.

Critical Concerns: Portraits often shows only portion of uniform worn and that is usually full dress as opposed to everyday wear; they are sometimes altered over time, as when a new decoration of the portrait subject is added after the fact; the uniform of the portrait subject may be atypical, as in the case of one officer who purchased a new uniform upon transfer to a new regiment and then had his portrait painted only to find that his tailor had made up a uniform of the old pattern and not the pattern then in use.[27]

8. Commercial prints of military subjects. The diverse items in this category vary widely in terms of their reliability, but the best provide a unique, although stylized, picture of the variety and colours of the uniforms worn during the period.

Examples: The Martinet Prints referred to in Note 10 above and those of C.-F. Weiland.[28]

Critical Concerns: Accuracy can be sacrificed to commercial considerations (e.g., the same basic print used to depict many different units, the only distinctions being in the colours of the facings); printing plates were often altered over time and prints from the same run might be coloured by different workmen, so there can be several variants of what is essentially one print; print subjects were sometimes drawn from hearsay rather than direct observation (e.g., one contemporary source includes a print of a 'British Lance Man' based on a proposal to raise such a unit which was ultimately rejected by the British government).[29]

9. Official uniform regulations and decrees. This source provides an important framework for much uniform research but can be very misleading if one assumes that exact compliance with regulations was the rule rather than the exception.

Examples: Dress information contained in the organizational decrees for particular units; administrative circulars reprinted in the *Journal Militaire.*[30]

Critical Concerns: Time lags in the implementation of regulations and lack of compliance with their specific terms (i.e., most Voltigeurs had a yellow collar and wore a sabre despite the existence of decrees requiring Voltigeurs to wear a chamois collar and forbidding them the use of the sabre); vocabulary can have different meanings in different contexts.

10. Personal memoirs. As a general rule, the usefulness of memoirs in research concerning military uniforms is a direct function of the amount of time that has elapsed between the dates described in the memoir and the date when the memoir was written. Hence, those recollections written shortly after the fall of Napoleon and those based on contemporaneous notes made by the authors tend to be the most helpful. Nevertheless, any passage in any memoir describing an incident that the author might have particular reason to remember accurately can offer valuable insight into matters of military dress and style (e.g., the use of fake moustaches and queues by insufficiently hirsute hussar recruits described by Marbot).[31]

Examples: Any work listed in Jean Tulard's extraordinarily useful compilation *Bibliographie Critique des Mémoires sur le Consulat et l'Empire* (Geneva, 1971–91).

Critical Concerns: Given the inherent fallibility of human memory, these sources must be used with extreme caution when other supporting evidence is unavailable.

We now turn to a detailed analysis of the individual paintings in the Manuscript. For this purpose the paintings have been divided into six groups roughly corresponding to the main organizational categories of troops in the Grand Army. Consideration of each group is preceded by a short explanatory note which provides background information about the types of troops depicted and their uniforms. The material in these notes is the foundation for the more detailed commentary that accompanies each painting.

A full list of all the paintings can be found in the Table of Contents. The list is based on precise translations of the captions which are hand-written on each of the paintings, but these have been supplemented by new material in brackets when it has been necessary correctly to identify a figure. The original Manuscript is not paginated, but the paintings have been numbered for the purposes of this study. The numbering generally, but not invariably, follows the order in which the paintings are bound. When two figures appear in the same painting, that on the left has been designated figure A and that on the right Figure B.

1   There is even confusion as to exactly when M. Depreaux's purchase of the Manuscript took place. Stiot's Article states that the drawings were acquired from a Leipzig bookseller named Hierseman 'shortly before the 1939 War'. That timing must be wrong, however, because one of the drawings, identified as a 'Contemporary German watercolour belonging to M. Albert Depreaux', had already been used by M. Depreaux to illustrate an article published in 1926. A. Depreaux, 'Les Gendarmes d'Ordonnance (24 Septembre 1806 – 23 Octobre 1807)', *Carnet de la Sabretache* (1926), pp. 540–543 (hereinafter Depreaux, 'Les Gendarmes d'Ordonnance').

2   Stiot's Article, at p. 47. These plates do not appear in the two standard reference works for French military prints, *Costumes Militaires – Catalogue des Principales Suites de Costumes Militaires Français Parues tant en France qu'à L'Étranger Depuis le Règne de Louis XV Jusqu'à nos Jours et des Suites de Costumes Militaires Étrangers Parues en France* (Paris 1900) by 'Un Membre de la Sabretache' [Otto von Glasser] (hereinafter referred to as 'Glasser') and Rene Colas, *Bibliographie Générale du Costume et de la Mode* (2 Vols., New York 1933). Intriguingly, however, Glasser, at p. 508, does contain a listing for a series of tableaux (including one of French cavalry and one of Russian cavalry) by a well-known German military artist named Wilhelm Kobell (1766–1855), who also executed a series of detailed paintings depicting the campaigns and battles of the Bavarian Army during the Napoleonic Wars. This coincidence suggests a possible confusion between the names Kolb and Kobell. For more information about the life and work of Kobell, see the entry for that artist in Ulrich Thieme and Felix Becker, *Allgemeines Lexikon Der Bildenden Kunstler*.

3   Rigo (b. 1925), official artist to the French Army, is the author of the famous *Le Plumet* series of uniform prints, each of which focuses on the uniform of a particular individual or unit and each of which is based on archival and other original sources.

4   See, e.g., Rousselot Plate No. 89: *Infanterie de Ligne –Têtes de Colonnes 1804–1812* (Paris 1965, reprinted 1981) (citing 'la suite d'aquarelles attribuée a Kolb') and *Le Plumet* No. 155: *Infanterie de Ligne – Sapeur des 8e, 14e, 18e Régiment 1805–1807* (citing 'Suite de Kolbe, dite Otto de Bade, Coll. Brown').

5   L. Rousselot, 'Infanterie 1807–1808', *Carnet de la Sabretache* (1972), p. 7.

6   See the article on the life and work of C. W. Kolbe 'the Younger' in *Allgemeines Lexikon Der Bildenden Kunstler*.

7   'Note de M. Depreaux sur le Recueil du Major Otto', *Carnet de la Sabretache* No. 27 (2nd Trimester 1975), pp. 47–49, at p. 47 (hereinafter 'Depreaux's Note'). Mrs. Brown's concurrence is evidenced by her use of the caption 'contemporary watercolour by an anonymous artist' to describe one of several Otto paintings which are reproduced in her adaptation and translation of Henry Lachouque's work on the Imperial Guard. Henry Lachouque, *The Anatomy of Glory* (Providence, Rhode Island 1962), Plate 58.

8   Stiot's Article states that the Manuscript as offered for sale to

9   This painting is reproduced as Plate 22: *Un Officier et Deux Grenadiers à Pied de la Garde Impériale en Tenue de Route, 1806–1807* in Jean Brunon, *Grenadiers de Napoléon* (n.l. [Marseilles], n.d. [1955]).

10 See Item No. 132 of the Catalogue from the exposition entitled 'Napoléon et la Grande Armée' presented by the Brunon Collection from 6 November to 31 December 1965.

11 Pierre de Hugo and Bertrand Malvaux, 'Les Bonnets à Poil des Grenadiers à Pied de la Garde Impériale', Pt. 1, *Tradition* No. 83 (December 1993), pp. 16–22, at 19 and front cover, and Pt. 2, *Tradition* No. 84 (January 1994), pp. 16–21 (hereinafter, Hugo and Malvaux, 'Les Bonnet à Poils'). The authors of this article clearly have only limited information about the Manuscript, however, because they state that they are aware of the existence of only a few original paintings from that series.

12 Hoffman worked from standardized plates but customized them using a heavy layer of colour to obscure the underlying printed design when necessary. Glasser, pp. 183–201.

13 The Martinet Plates are a series of some 296 prints of French military figures which are the work of a number of different artists and which were published by Aaron Martinet (1762–1841) between 1807 and 1815 under the title *Troupes Françaises*. Louis Hautecoeur, 'Une Famille de Graveurs et d'Editeurs Parisiens: Les Martinets et les Hautecoeurs (XVIII et XIX Siècles)', *Paris et Ile-de-France: Mémoires*, Vol. 18–19, pp. 205–340 (1967–68). (Contrary to popular belief, there is no known connection between the Martinet prints and the French artist Pierre Martinet (1781–1845?).) A list of the full run of prints can be found in Glasser, at pp. 299–313.

14 The history of this unit is given in A. Depreaux, 'Les Gendarmes d'Ordonnance'. See also L. Fallou, *La Garde Impériale* (Paris and Krefeld, Germany 1901 and 1975), pp. 361–365 (hereinafter 'Fallou'). Fallou's work is technically only a secondary source, but it is extraordinarily valuable as a convenient compilation of primary information about the organization and uniforms of Napoleon's Guard.

15 On the creation of the Fusiliers, see the introductory text to Part I (and the relevant note).

16 See the discussion of the white uniform in the introductory text to Part II.

17 Schobert's order book for the 3rd Regiment from 1806–1808 (hereinafter referred to as 'Schobert's Order Book') is quoted from extensively in Lucien Rousselot, 'Troupes Françaises en Allemagne 1807–1808', *Carnet de la Sabretache* (1972), pp. 40–42 (hereinafter Rousselot, 'Troupes Françaises').

18 For instance, Albrecht Adam (1786–1862), a Bavarian military painter, compiled (under the deceptively bucolic title, *Voyage Pittoresque et Militaire de Willenberg en Prusse jusqu à Moscou fait en 1812* (Munich 1827–30)) an illustrated record of his participation in the first half of the Russian Campaign in which the subject of each illustration is dated and described by the artist. He also left a more general account of his campaigns attached to the staff of Prince Eugène Beauharnais, the Viceroy of the Kingdom of Italy, which provided the subject matter for most of his military works. Albrecht Adam, *Aus den Leben eines Schlachtenmaler* (Stuttgart 1886).

19 For the history of the Rovatti Chronicle, see Giancarlo Boeri's 'La Cronaca Rovatti', a special publication of *Revista Militare Europea* (May–June 1989). The Chronicle itself can be found in the Municipal Archives of the City of Modena in Italy. Many of the Rovatti illustrations of French soldiers have been analysed by Rigo in his article 'Ceux de Marengo' in *Tradition* Nos. 30–31 (July/August 1989), pp. 32–45.

20 One of Ornstrup's paintings is reproduced in colour in Lars Lindeberg, *De sa det ske Englandskrigene 1801–1815* (Copenhagen 1974), pp. 164–165. The originals are in the Royal Danish Library in Copenhagen.

21 A photograph of this plate appears in Christian Blondieau's invaluable reference work, *Aigles et Shakos du Premier Empire* (Paris 1980), p. 33 (hereinafter referred to as 'Blondieau, *Aigles et Shakos*').

22 Vicomte de Boislecomte, 'Les Souvenirs du Lieutenant-Colonel Boucquel de Beauval 1804–1830', *Carnet de la Sabretache* Vol. 5 (1897), pp. 298–309, at 301 (hereinafter referred to as 'Beauval, *Souvenirs*'). This source is quoted in Depreaux's Note, but the year of publication is incorrectly given as 1906. It is referenced in Ronald J. Caldwell, *The Era of Napoleon: A Bibliography of the History of Western Civilization, 1799–1815* (2 vols., New York 1991), Vol. 1, p. 349, but not in Jean Tulard, *Bibliographie Critique de Mémoires* (Geneva 1971), which instead under the alphabetical listing of 'Beauval' notes only the portion of Boucquel de Beauval's memoirs which relate to his captivity in England. See 'Treize Mois de Captivité', *Le Correspondant* Vol. 168 (1892), pp. 1135–1148.

23 These materials are the subject of a two part article by Rigo and George Englebrecht entitled 'Albrecht Adam et les Grognards' in *Uniformes* No. 91 (November/December 1985), pp. 11–16, and No. 96 (July/August 1986), pp. 37–39. For general information about the artist, see Note 22 above.

24 This manuscript is generally considered to be the work of a Hamburg native named Christoph Suhr (1771–1842). The provenance of this source is complicated, but the original paintings are apparently those which can now be found in the Lipperheide Costume Library in Berlin. They are numbered and indexed in Glasser, pp. 173–179.

25 The Zimmerman drawings, which can also be found in the Brown Collection, are a numbered set of finely detailed (but somewhat awkward) pen and ink drawings with captions which are signed 'Zimmerman fecit 1808'. The set has a title page with the legend 'Costume des Troupes Françaises & de celles de L'Alliance du Rhin qui ont étés à Berlin depuis le 24 Octobre 1806', and thus illustrates figures from the same period as the Otto Manuscript. These works are not listed in Glasser. Some modern facsimiles of these drawings have been coloured, but these coloured versions should not be considered reliable.

26 Napoleon I, *Correspondance de Napoléon 1er; Publiée par Ordre de L'Empereur Napoléon III* (32 Vols., Paris 1858–1870).

27 Francois Dumonceau, *Mémoires du Général Comte François Dumonceau, publiés d'après le manuscrit original par Jean Puraye*, (3 vols., Brussels 1958–1963), vol. 2, pp. 273–274 and 277–78 (hereinafter referred to as 'Dumonceau, *Mémoires*').

28 Weiland was an ex-Captain of the Württemberg Army who produced a commercial set of some 148 coloured uniform engravings in two editions (1807 and 1812) (hereinafter referred to as the 'Weiland Plates'). The Weiland Plates, which are not individually numbered, are indexed in Glasser, pp.415–420.

29 See Plate No. 27 in T. Goddard and J. Booth, *The Military Costume of Europe* (London 1822).

30 The *Journal Militaire*, or to use its full name, *Journal Militaire, contenant tout ce qui est relatif à la Composition et à l'Administration de la Force Publique, et enfin tout qui concerne la Guerre et la Marine* (Paris), was the publication used to circulate all official regulations, decrees and correspondance relating to the military administration of the French army.

31 Jean-Baptiste Marbot, *The Memoirs of Baron de Marbot* (Arthur John Butler, trans.; London 1893), p. 36. The scene remembered by Marbot has been captured visually in an amusing nineteenth century painting reproduced in Alain Pigeard, 'A La Hussarde!', *Tradition* No. 66–67 (July/August 1992), pp. 17–21, at 20.

PART I
THE IMPERIAL GUARD

PART I
THE IMPERIAL GUARD

The military institution identified more than any other with the reign of Napoleon is, of course, his personal Guard, embodied first as the small Consular Guard and then transformed into the Imperial Guard in 1804. At the start of the Jena campaign, it was still a relatively modest formation of all arms, so much so that the familiar division of the constituent units into Old, Middle and Young Guard had not yet become necessary. It had, however, already become the epitome of an élite corps.

The spiritual and physical centre of the Guard was provided by two regiments of foot Grenadiers and two of foot Chasseurs, each consisting of eight companies of 120 men divided into two battalions.[1] Dressed in their elegant blue and white uniforms, complete with signature bearskin cap and epaulettes, these soldiers, veterans all, are among the most familiar, and evocative, iconographic images of the First Empire.[2] As faithfully recorded by the Otto Manuscript, however, the Guard infantry also had a simpler campaign uniform. Each company of infantry included two soldiers designated as Sappers who were distinguished by virtue of the fact that they typically had beards, wore a long leather apron and were equipped with axes as well as muskets.[3] These specialists, who ranked as corporals, had both practical and ceremonial roles to play. In combat or on campaign, the Sappers were available to clear natural obstacles from the path of their unit. On parade, marching with axes unsheathed, they

enhanced the martial image of their units by their primitive, warlike appearance.

Even early in his reign, however, Napoleon found that he had to resort to creative strategies to fulfil his manpower needs. Thus, by 1806, the Guard infantry also contained two regiments of volunteer trainees (each of which had two battalions), one called the Grenadier Vélites, the other the Chasseur Vélites.[4] By a decree of 19 September 1806, the first battalions of these two regiments were transformed into a new unit called simply the Vélites' of the Guard, which was filled out with the rank and file from the second battalions and attached to the corps of Guard Grenadiers. The cadres of the two second battalions meanwhile were combined with conscripts to form a new unit designated the 'Fusiliers' of the Guard which was attached for administrative purposes to the corps of Guard Chasseurs. By virtue of a subsequent decree dated 15 December 1806, the Fusiliers, commanded by Colonel Boyer de Rebeval, now became the first Fusilier Regiment or Fusilier-Chasseurs; the Vélites under the command of Colonel Friedrichs became the second Fusilier Regiment or Fusilier-Grenadiers.[5]

The cavalry of the Guard consisted of both so-called heavy and light units. The Mounted Grenadiers, Mounted Chasseurs and Dragoons were all full regiments subdivided into four squadrons of two companies each, each company being 124 men strong.[6] The Mamelukes, on the other hand, were simply an overstrength company attached for administrative purposes to the Mounted Chasseurs.[7] Each of these units wore a distinctive uniform, but in all cases (except for that of the Mamelukes) there was liberal use of *aurore* cords and trim. There was also a common tendency for the units to cloth their trumpeters in coats of sky-blue and crimson. The Mounted Chasseurs may have been Napoleon's favourites, judging from the fact that he often wore the undress uniform of an officer of that regiment, but the Mounted Grenadiers seem to have held a slight edge in dignity and prestige because of their unit seniority and the similarities between their uniforms and those of the foot Grenadiers. The Dragoons were only a recent addition to the Guard, having been created early in 1806, but they had already caught the eye of Josephine and become (unofficially) the Dragoons of the Empress. The Mamelukes were ostensibly all natives of the Ottoman Empire who had accompanied the French army back from its occupation of Egypt, but attrition had already caused some Europeans to be added to the ranks.

Another distinguishing feature of most Guard cavalry uniforms was an aiguillette, or set of ornamental cords suspended from the wearer's shoulder. The historical origins of this decorative item are obscure, but aiguillettes have long been used as a badge of rank or élite status. During the Napoleonic era they seem to have consistently taken the form of a shoulderpiece, two equal-sized, single-strand loops of cord and two braided end pieces of unequal length fitted with decorative metal tips.[8] The two free ends (the longer one looped under the arm) and one of the loops were invariably connected to buttons or buttonholes (sources differ on this detail) on the front of the jacket to create the characteristic aiguillette pattern of decoration.

Because the Imperial Guard was genuinely an army in miniature, its strength also included artillery and support formations. The most important of these was a three squadron regiment of Horse Artillery, clothed in the traditional artillery colours of blue and red, which was supported by a battalion strength Artillery Train.[9] Also mounted, but with more limited combat functions, were the four companies of Elite Gendarmes.[10] The normal campaign strength of the Guard was completed by a Baggage Train Battalion, a battalion of Administrative Workers and a unit of Sailors divided into five 'crews'.[11]

The *Gendarmes d'Ordonnance*, or Gendarme Orderlies, were created by Napoleon even while he was occupied with the task of defeating the Prussian armies at Jena and Auerstadt. They constituted a unique experiment conducted by him for the purpose of solving two chronic problems of his regime: that of attracting the upper classes of France to the ranks of his adherents and that of providing a continuing source of skilled cavalry officers to make good the continual attrition in the ranks of his mounted troops. Membership in the unit was thus limited to men from rich aristocratic families and each recruit was informed that he had a good prospect of being posted as an officer in a line cavalry regiment upon satisfactory completion of only a single campaign with the army.[12] The concentration of privilege represented by the Gendarmes excited such jealousy within the Guard and the army that the unit had to be disbanded in 1807, although the concept which the Gendarmes embodied was revived again in 1813 and 1814 with the Honour Guards.

The Imperial Guard as an institution serves to demonstrate that Napoleon was a master of motivational as well as military strategy – he instinctively grasped the profound truth that men can be made to perform extraordinary feats of valour by appeals to their vanity. Napoleon's supreme creation in this regard was the Legion of Honour, a chivalric order founded in 1804 to give visible recognition to the new aristocracy of courageous and devoted soldiers produced by the turmoil of the Revolution and the Consulate. 'It is with baubles such as these that men are led,' Napoleon is said to have cynically remarked, and there is no denying the remarkable heroic feats accomplished by French soldiers in quest of the 'Cross' of the Legion (which, ironically, was not a cross at all).[13] Twenty-two of the figures illustrated in the Manuscript are wearing either a full decoration of the Legion or a short length of red ribbon, the latter being a customary way of signifying membership in the Legion without exposing the Cross itself to the hazards of life on campaign.

Along these same motivational lines, Napoleon also tried to give recognition to his veteran soldiers by awarding them increased pay and a distinctive insignia. The latter consisted of red woollen chevrons worn on the left sleeve; one chevron signifying ten years' service, two fifteen, and three identifying a twenty-year soldier.[14] It is very surprising that none of the Otto figures have these long-service stripes.

1 See Imperial Decree of 16 April 1806 cited in Fallou, p. 85.

2 Soldiers had to have at least five years' service before they could be admitted to the Guard. Fallou, p. 88.
3 The term 'Sapper' originally applied specifically to soldiers whose specialty was the digging of saps, or siege trenches, but it eventually came to encompass any soldier equipped with an axe or other tool.
4 Henri Lachouque, 'Les Vélites de la Garde Impériale', *Revue de la Société des Amis du Musée de l'Armée* No. 64 (1961), pp. 41–52.
5 There is general agreement as to the basic elements of this complicated sequence of events, but disagreement as to which of the two Fusilier regiments came to be associated with the corps of Grenadiers since, despite secondary source assertions to the contrary, the text of the 15 December decree set forth in Arthur Chuquet, ed., *Ordres et Apostilles de Napoléon (1799–1815)* (4 Vols., Paris 1911–12), Vol. 3, p. 156, is ambiguous on this point. This work adopts the conclusion of Lachouque (see Note 4 above) and Rousselot (Plate No. 101: *Fusiliers de la Garde 1806–1814* (Paris 1968)) that the second Fusilier regiment formed from the Vélites became the Fusilier-Grenadiers.
6 Fallou, pp. 195–197, 212 and 241.
7 Fallou, pp. 237–238.
8 The details of construction of an aiguillette are clearly shown in the line drawing of a Guard Lancer aiguillette which can be found in Fallou, p. 278.
9 Fallou, pp. 312 and 351.
10 Fallou, pp. 305 and 362.
11 Fallou, pp. 312, 355 and 358.
12 Frederic Masson, *Cavaliers de Napoléon* (Paris 1896), pp. 95–102.
13 The decoration consisted of a white star (formed by adding a fifth arm to the shape of a Maltese cross) with a gold bust of the Emperor on its obverse surrounded by a blue border bearing in gold letters the legend 'Napoléon Emp. des Français'. A wreath of green laurel leaves was visible between the rays of the star. In all the Otto paintings the medal is attached to the obligatory red ribbon by a gold crown, although this feature did not appear on the earliest versions of the medal. See R.D. Stiot's article 'L'Ordre de la Légion d'Honneur – Ses Insignes', *Tradition* No. 25 (February 1989), pp. 26–30. (This French language *Tradition*, which has set new standards of excellence for articles on military uniforms by virtue of its presentation of copious photographic reproductions of relevant artwork and artefacts, should not be confused with the now-defunct English journal of the same name.)
14 See the circular of 3 Thermidor Year 10 (22 July 1802) reprinted in Captain P.-C. Alombert, *Le Corps d'armée aux ordres du Maréchal Mortier* (Paris 1987), pp. 318–319 (hereinafter 'Alombert, *Le Corps du Mortier*').

1
Untitled [French Marshal]

The identification of this figure is not entirely free from doubt, but it seems probable that the uniform illustrated is that of a Marshal of the Empire, and it is even possible that the painting represents a portrait of Marshal Jean-de-Dieu Soult.[1] The undress uniforms of the French Marshals and Divisional Generals during the Napoleonic period were almost identical, the chief distinguishing features of the former being white and gold waist sashes and white feather edging on the hat, as well as the variety and number of medals and other decorations worn.[2] Since the figure illustrated is not wearing a waist sash at all (that omission being perhaps the most novel sartorial point presented by the painting), the trim on the hat becomes the decisive identifying feature. The grand cordon of the Legion of Honour worn under the coat, and the blue breeches are two other noteworthy points about this figure. The straight sword is a surprising accessory because mounted officers almost invariably were armed with a curved sabre.

The possible connection of this figure with Marshal Soult is suggested by a statement which appears in M. Depreaux's description of the Otto Manuscript.[3] He asserts that one of the decorations worn by the figure is the Cross of the Order of Saint Hubert of Bavaria and that Marshal Soult was the only general officer in the Grand Army authorized to wear that medal at the time in question. Soult was certainly a member of that chivalric order (as well as several others), but the author of this work has been able to verify independently neither the identification of the medal nor the assertion of Soult's unique right to wear it. The face of the figure is not inconsistent with the portrait of Marshal Soult by Louis-Henri Rudder (1807–81) at Versailles (copying an earlier, now missing, portrait by Jean Broc (1780–1850)), but that painting also shows Soult wearing an aiguillette (shoulder cords) on his right shoulder as a symbol of his honorary rank as the Colonel-General of the Foot Chasseurs of the Imperial Guard, a distinction which is missing here.

1 A new biography of Marshal Soult, the first ever in English, reproduces a copy of his birth certificate and thus proves once and for all that his first name was not 'Nicolas'. See Sir Peter Hayman, *Soult, Napoleon's Maligned Marshal* (London 1990), illustration opposite p. 96.
2 See the Decree of 26 Fructidor, Year XII (13 September 1804) concerning the dress of Marshals (reprinted in the text accompanying Rousselot Plate No. 100: *Maréchaux d'Empire (1804–1815)* (Paris 1967/1982). See also Georges Six, *Les Généraux de la Révolution et de L'Empire* (Lyon 1948), p. 146.
3 See Depreaux's Note, at p. 48.

2
Sapper of the Foot Grenadiers of the Guard

This Sapper, with his flowing beard and fear-some axe, is the model of an imposing warrior. For the most part, his uniform is unexceptional in that it is consistent with accepted descriptions of Sapper dress, including the wearing of a bearskin cap without a cap plate. The painting does, however, present a few bits of new information for consideration which contradict the traditional view: (1) the cords on the bearskin are white (silver?) and red instead of gold and red; (2) the specialist badge on the sleeve of the uniform has red axes on a gold background instead of gold on red (although Rousselot states that the former design was standard for the undress uniform)[1]; (3) the sabre's hilt has a single-branch guard which seems to indicate that it is a standard infantry model 'briquet' and not the combination sabre/saw for Sappers with a distinctive hilt in the shape of the head of a rooster shown by most sources.[2] The epaulettes in full dress would have had gold crescents and stripes, but the plain red version shown here is appropriate for campaign wear. The cockade lacks the superimposed eagle which was introduced after 1807, another circumstance which provides clues for dating the Manuscript.

The most novel aspect of this figure is the arrangement of his belts and equipment. As a matter of common sense, given that the cartridge box (which appears to be an exact but reduced version of the standard Guard grenadier box) is worn on the waistbelt, one of the two belts worn over the left shoulder must be for the short musket (which appears to be slung under the knapsack) and one must be for the axe case. Assuming that the musket strap is the narrower of the two belts, it is surprising to find the wider belt for the axe case unadorned, especially since the belt for the sabre bears the traditional brass Sapper devices of a Medusa's head and crossed axes. In Martinet Plate No. 120 of a Guard Grenadier Sapper in full dress, the Medusa device is found on both belts, and the surviving example of a belt in the French Army Museum is ornamented with no less than three brass devices: a Medusa, a grenade and a set of crossed axes.[3] The sweep of the axe blade is extreme and does not look as though it would have fitted in any surviving example of case.

---

1 Rousselot Plate No. 63: *Grenadiers à Pied de la Garde –Tête de Colonne 1800–1815* (Paris 1958/1980); but see, to the contrary, Fallou pp. 105–106.
2 Fallou, p. 117.
3 Paul Willing, *Napoléon et ses Soldats* (2 Vols., Paris 1986–87), Vol. 1 (*L'Apogée de la Gloire*), p. 42 (hereinafter referred to as 'Willing, Vol. 1'). This work is essentially an illustrated catalogue of artefacts in the French Army Museum, and is one of the most useful modern sources of information about Napoleon's armies.

3
Drummer of the Foot Guard

The uniform shown in this painting conforms very closely to the known regulations, which prescribed essentially the same campaign dress for the drummers as for ordinary Grenadiers, but with gold trim on the collar and cuffs.[1] The bearskin is the standard troop model with metal plate, an imposing headpiece which, according to the then Private Jean Coignet, was large enough to double as a carrying case for two bottles of wine.[2] The bearskin is so drawn that enough of the backpatch is visible to confirm that it takes the form of a white cross on a red ground, and not the form of a white grenade, the ornament that was introduced after the return from the 1807 campaign, thus providing further evidence for dating the Manuscript.[3] The striped item above the rolled greatcoat on his pack is probably the case for the bearskin. A surprise here is the pointed shape of the cuffs, which is more consistent with the style of cuff on the uniform of the Guard Chasseurs than with the square cuffs on the dress uniform of the Grenadiers. A typical Otto detail is the fact that the figure is wearing the characteristic gold earring of the true 'grognard' or 'grumbler'.[4]

Despite the omnipresence of drummers throughout the Grand Army, there are very few certifiably contemporary depictions of Napoleonic drums themselves. All are in accord that the shell of the drum was brass and had cords for adjusting the surface tension of the head, but most depict the rims as being medium blue and not tri-coloured, as in this case.[5] This painting also shows clearly the brass drum stick holder on the belt supporting the drum, and the two straps below the drum which could be used to carry the instrument on the drummer's back when a pack was not being worn.

1 See, e.g., Rousselot Plate No. 63.
2 Speaking of the night before the Battle of Jena, Coignet writes: 'There was a great quantity of it [wine]; each grenadier had three bottles, two in his bear-skin cap, and one in his pocket.' *The Narrative of Captain Coignet (Soldier of the Empire) 1776–1850* (Mrs. M. Carey, trans.; New York 1890), p. 132.
3 Fallou, p. 100–101.
4 'The particular trademark of the style of the Guard grenadier was the gold earring; it was, de rigueur, his first purchase on joining the corps.' Hyacinthe-Hippolyte de Mauduit, *Les Derniers Jours de la Grande Armée, ou, Souvenirs, documens et correspondance inédite de Napoléon en 1814 et 1815* (2 vols., Paris 1847–48) Vol. 1, p. 455.
5 See, e.g., Martinet Plate No. 161: *Infanterie de Ligne –Tambour battant la Diane.*

Tambour de la Garde à pie.

4
Officer of the Foot Guard

This figure is clearly an officer of the Grenadiers of the Guard and, based on the arrangement and detail of his epaulettes, his rank is most likely that of Captain. His bearskin, together with all the others depicted in the Manuscript, has an unnaturally smooth and curved profile and the upper end of the visible cap cord should probably be on the right, and not the left, side of the peak tassel because it is supposed to connect with the flat oval 'flounders' (raquettes) hanging at the right side of the cap.[1] As appropriate for an officer, the cords are gold and, based on the glimpse of the backpatch provided by the artist (contrary to all rules of perspective), there even appears to be some gold ornamentation on the white cross at the rear of the head-dress. The cap plate lacks the two small grenades flanking the eagle which are visible in the other Guard cap plates illustrated in the Manuscript, but it is unclear whether this is another officer's distinction or merely an omission by the artist.[2] The single-breasted jacket, which is the predominant dress for officers throughout the Manuscript, seems to have more than its fair share of breast buttons; there are ten showing and room for one more under the gorget even though the successive dress regulations up to 1807 called for, respectively, only seven, eight and nine buttons. (On the other hand, the jacket surprisingly has no buttons at all visible near the cuff opening.) The gorget, with its silver eagle ornament surrounded by what appears to be a wreath of laurel and oak leaves, is of interest because this picture provides one of the few contemporary illustrations of this piece of Guard equipment.[3] The black sword belt seems an unusual touch for a Guard officer, but a similar belt (though with red edging) is shown in the plate of a Grenadier officer in the 1808 edition of the Weiland Plates. The square gold belt plate with silver eagle is also a detail not found in other sources. The breeches and boots conform to regulations, but the brown 'cuffs' of the latter appear to have exaggerated dimensions.

This figure also provides two fine examples of the exquisite detail which the Otto artist was capable of depicting, one being the cross of the Legion of Honour worn by the officer and the other the decorative metal work on the blade of the sabre.

1   See generally the photographs of surviving Guard bearskins in Hugo and Malvaux, 'Les Bonnets à Poil'. The bearskins could apparently have either one or two raquettes. *Ibid.*, Pt. 2, p. 20.
2   Fallou, p. 111.
3   Fallou, p. 111. A photograph of an example of this type of Guard Grenadier gorget can be found in Willing, Vol. 2 (*De Wagram à Waterloo 1809–1815*), p. 14 (hereinafter referred to as 'Willing, Vol. 2').

Officier de la   Garde à pié.

5
Foot Grenadiers of the Guard

The composition of this painting is atypical for the Manuscript because it shows the same uniform in both front and back views. (The second figure is apparently a different soldier because the title refers to 'Grenadiers' in the plural.) The uniform depicted in the front view is confirmed in nearly all details by a print by the German artist Wilhelm Hendschel (1781–1865) bearing the title 'Grenadier à pied de la garde Imp[ériale]. et Roy[ale].' published in Berlin in 1807, although the latter does clearly show red piping on the collar.[1] The back view (together with that in the subsequent picture of the Guard Chasseurs) is one of the few contemporary pictures that depict clearly the arrangement of the equipment carried by the typical French infantryman of the Napoleonic period. One can make out not only the hairy exterior of the standard French knapsack (made from the pelt of a goat or a cow), but even the blue fatigue cap with red tassel strapped to the bottom of the cartridge box. Given the lack of ornamentation elsewhere on the jacket, it is perhaps surprising to find the pockets in the tails trimmed in red, but this feature is confirmed by the Weiland Plate of a Guard Grenadier. Note how poorly the aurore (orange) grenades show up against the scarlet background of the turnbacks. The black gaiters should have brass buttons, but theses seem to be black in this case. The skill of the Otto artist in rendering details is manifest in the way he depicts even the stitching just inside each edge of the belting which was a standard feature of all Old Guard leatherwork.[2] (Belts with this feature were worn only rarely by Line troops.) The white sabre strap (a length of leather which theoretically was used to attach the hilt of the sabre to the wrist of the soldier in combat to prevent accidental loss of the weapon, but which basically played only an ornamental role for an infantryman) with red tassel is also carefully detailed down to the precise way in which the strap was wrapped around the hilt when not in use.

1 Hendschel created a total of twelve prints of French Army figures in 1807 and they constitute one of the premier sources of information about the dress of the Imperial Guard during the Prussian Campaign. For a complete list of the prints, see Glasser, p. 181. These are the only known military prints by that artist.
2 Rousselot Plate No. 40: *Grenadiers à pied de la Garde 1800–1815* (Paris 1943/1978). See also, Michel Pétard, 'L'Homme de 1807 – Le Grenadier à pied de la Vieille Garde', *Uniformes* No. 38 (July/August 1977), pp. 18–27, one instalment of a superb series of articles about French uniforms in the period covered by the Otto Manuscript. M. Pétard is an accomplished illustrator in his own right, but his articles are also valuable because he generally provides reproductions of key primary sources.

Grenadiers   *à pié*   *de la Garde*

6
Sapper of the Chasseurs of the Foot Guard

Except for relatively minor points of detail, the uniform of the Sapper of the Guard Chasseurs is identical with that of his colleague of the Guard Grenadiers. The main differences can be found in the head-dress, where the cording is green and white instead of red and white, and the plume is green and red. For the rest, the epaulettes have a green shoulder piece, the double axe sleeve badge is edged with green and the corners of the cartridge box are adorned with the characteristic bugle horn of the Chasseurs instead of the grenade of the Grenadiers. The similarities with the Grenadier Sapper also extend to equipment. The belts have identical decorations and, once again, the cartridge box is worn 'Corsican-style' on a waistbelt, a location rarely shown in Napoleonic iconography but which was the official alternative to the cartridge box being located on the axe case.[1] The series by Hendschel also contains a plate depicting a 'Chasseur Sappeur à pied' whose uniform differs from the one depicted here in the use of mixed gold, green and red cords on the bearskin and a single shoulder belt and the lack of the cartridge box worn over the stomach, but since the Hendschel figure bears the chevrons of a corporal, these differences may simply represent rank distinctions.

The axe blade is even larger than that of the Grenadier Sapper and the poll has been shaped into a threatening, but non-utilitarian, hooked blade. The combination of these features would seemingly have made for an unwieldy instrument which would require an exceptionally large carrying case. He is also armed with a standard infantry model sabre. The artist has clearly detailed the buckle which was used to secure the sabre scabbard in place after it was inserted in the white leather frog on the shoulderbelt, but the picture fails to show that the one end of the strap inserted in the buckle would have come from the scabbard through a slit in the leather.[2] The predominantly green tassel on the sabre strap has only a small ring of red.

1 See letter of the Minister of War dated 11 Fructidor An 12 cited in *Manuel d'Infanterie, ou résumé de tous les Reglemens, Decrets, Usages, et Renseignements propres aux Sous-Officiers de cette arme* (Paris 1813), p. 81 (hereinafter referred to as '*Manuel d'Infanterie*').
2 This complex, but practical, arrangement is usefully illustrated by a series of drawings on page 23 of Michel Pétard, *Équipements Militaires de 1600 à 1870*, Vol. 4 – *de 1804 à 1815 (Première partie)* (Olonne-sur-Mer, France 1987) (hereinafter referred to as 'Pétard, *Équipements Militaires*').

7

Foot Chasseurs of the Guard

The term 'Chasseur' (literally, 'hunter') was used in the French Army to designate both infantry and cavalry units capable of carrying out skirmishing functions, but by 1806 the designation had lost most of its practical significance. What remained was the use of green as a distinctive colour and hunting-horns as a distinctive insignia. The undress uniform depicted in this painting is therefore quite similar to that of the Grenadiers, but with the characteristic differences of the two-coloured plume, the green shoulder-strap for the epaulettes, the hunting-horn ornament substituted for one of the grenades in the turnbacks of the jacket, and the green tassel on the sabre strap.[1] The most obvious difference between the uniforms of the Guard Grenadiers and the Guard Chasseurs, however, was the absence of a cap plate on the Chasseur bearskins.

The artist seems to have depicted some novelties in the dress of these Chasseurs. Rousselot is emphatic that the Chasseur bearskin had two tassels at its peak, and not one as depicted here, and he is equally explicit that the hunting-horn device appeared in the exterior and not the interior turnback.[2] Hendschel's 1807 print of a 'Chasseur Grenadier à pied de la garde Imp[ériale]. et Roy[ale].' shows the same arrangement of turnback ornaments as Rousselot, but has red trim on the green epaulette shoulder-strap and collar, and a completely red tassel on the sabre strap. The eagle facing left instead of right on the cartridge box is most likely an error rather than a novelty, but the artist is correct in showing the cartridge box as otherwise unadorned, unlike that of the Chasseur Sapper.[3] The shoulder-strap frog for the sabre lacks the requisite buckle, and the scabbard for the bayonet seems unnaturally short.

It is believed that all Guard infantrymen had long hair worn gathered in a queue, but this point can neither be confirmed nor denied on the basis of the relevant Otto pictures because none of them permits a clear view of the back of a Guardsman's head.

---

1   See generally, Michel Pétard, 'L'Homme de 1807 – Le Chasseur à Pied de la Garde', *Uniformes* No. 81 (March/April 1984), pp. 10–13.
2   Rousselot Plate No. 58: *Chasseurs à Pied de la Garde 1800–1815* (Paris 1957). The detail of the tassels is also shown clearly in Martinet Plate No. 107: *Officiers de Chasseurs de la Garde Impériale* and there is a surviving bearskin of a Chasseur NCO in the French Army Museum in Paris which has that same feature.
3   Fallou, p. 157.

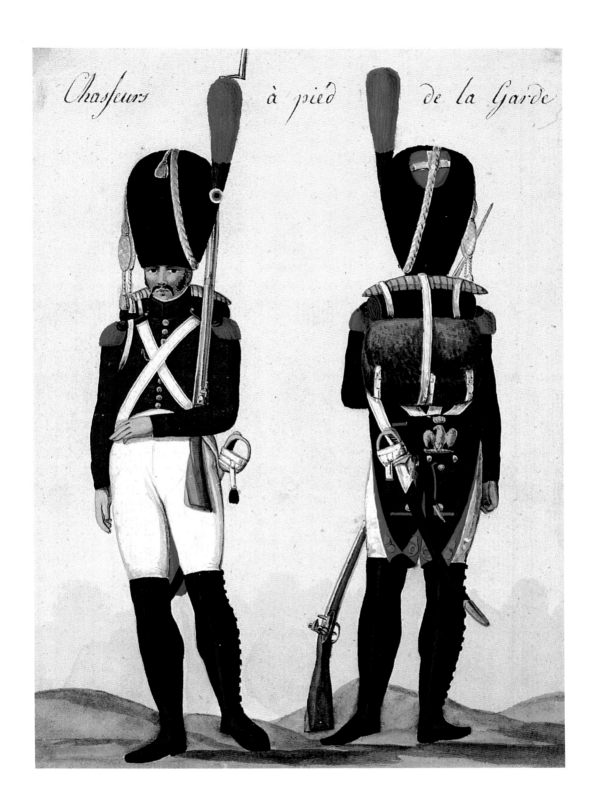

Chasfeurs   à pied   de la Garde

8
Fusilier[-Grenadier] of the Guard

This Otto painting is the only known primary source that shows the original uniform of the Fusilier-Grenadiers formed in December of 1806 from the Regiment of Guard Vélites.[1] Although the caption to the painting does not specify which of the two regiments of Fusiliers is depicted, the red plume, white shako chevrons and the straight cuffs with cuff flaps are all features that appear in sources that indisputably illustrate later versions of the Fusilier-Grenadier uniform.[2] The only point not consistent with this identification is that the lower edge of the jacket lapels ends in a point and not in a square, a feature more consistent with the style of dress worn by the Fusilier-Chasseurs.[3] Nevertheless, a reasonable possibility exists that the detail of the pointed lapels is correct. The Guard Vélites which were transformed into the Fusilier-Grenadiers had one battalion of Grenadier Vélites and one battalion of Chasseur Vélites, each of which wore essentially the same uniform as its 'parent' corps.[4] The Fusilier-Grenadiers may therefore initially have had one battalion with pointed lapels and the other with square lapels and the process of tailoring consistent uniform jackets could have been delayed for some time by the unit's participation in active campaigning. The use of shoulder-straps rather than epaulettes is in keeping both with the Fusilier designation and with Napoleon's stated purpose of saving money by turning the Vélites into a unit with lower operating costs. The blue colour of the straps and their red piping can also be found in a Hoffman painting of a Vélite and thus logically appear in this painting as well. (The placement of the button of the shoulder-strap on the end of the strap away from the neck is atypical, but not unprecedented, as discussed in the text to Plate No. 30 below.) The shako with brass eagle plate and white leather trim and cords is closely identified with both regiments of Fusiliers, but the white upper band and the suggestion of a third white vertical stripe in the angle of the other two are both unique, as is the red colour of the cuff-flap and the existence of brass buttons on the flap of the waistcoat pocket. The other equipment of this figure is accurately depicted from his musket to his gaiter buttons.

1   See Note 5 and accompanying text in Part I.
2   See, e.g., Martinet Plate No. 62, reproduced in Michel Pétard, 'L'Homme de 1807 – Le Fusilier-Grenadier de la Garde' in *Uniformes* No. 98 (November 1986), pp. 24–29, at 24.
3   See Weiland's Plate of a Fusilier-Chasseur reproduced in Michel Pétard, 'Les Fusiliers de la Garde Impériale (Moyenne Garde)', *Tradition,* No. 83 (December 1993), pp. 10–15, at 14.
4   See Glasser, p. 196.

Fusilier de la Garde

9
Naval Soldiers [Sailors of the Guard]

Although at various times several different naval formations served with the Grand Army, there can be no doubt that the figures illustrated here represent members of the battalion of Sailors of the Imperial Guard[1] because the undress uniform depicted agrees in almost all respects with that displayed in the other contemporary illustrations of this unit by the Bourgeois of Hamburg, Weiland, Zimmerman and Berka. The Otto painting is, nevertheless, sufficiently unique in some details to create an array of uniform enigmas. Based on the iconographic sources noted above and existing head-dresses in the collections of the French Army Museum, it seems that the first model of shako worn by the Guard Sailors had a removable visor and did not have a cap plate of any sort beneath the cockade (and its orange retaining strap) at the front of the shako.[2] This eventually gave way to a second model which also had a removable visor, but which now had a cap plate in front and a cockade attached by cords on the left side of the shako.[3] The model recorded by the Otto artist appears to fall between these other two because the visor appears to be fixed to the shako, but the cockade appears above the eagle plate (note that the eagle should be facing to the right and not the left). The Otto example may therefore be either an interim official Guard model or perhaps a Line shako adopted for temporary Guard use. Three other anomalous features depicted by the Otto artist are the black straps for the pack, the blue/black (?) crescent at the outer edge of the brass epaulettes and the curved sabre which lacks the rounded single-branch guard and sword knot shown in all other sources. The belt plate with anchor is an accurate depiction of the earliest model of this item of equipment.[4]

1   There is often confusion as to the correct name of this unit, which is perhaps understandable given that the decree creating the battalion refers to both *matelots* (sailors) and *marins* (seamen), but the former term more accurately describes the intended role of these troops. Dr. Eugène Lomier, *Le Bataillon des Marins de la Garde* (St-Valéry-Sur-Somme 1905), pp. 30–31.
2   See Hendschel's print of a '*Marin de la garde Impl. et Royl.*' and plates 90 and 91 of the Bourgeois of Hambourg Collection.
3   Photographs of an existing example of this model can be found in Willing, Vol. 1, p. 65, and a helpful painting of what is probably the same shako appears in Plate CXCI of the Album Volume of H. Malibran's *Guide à L'Usage des Artistes et des Costumiers . . .* (2 Vols., Paris 1904–1907).
4   Bertrand Malvaux, 'Les Plaques de Ceinturon des Marins de la Garde Impériale', *Tradition* No. 60 (January 1992), pp. 17–20.

Soldats

de la marine

de la garde

10
Trumpeter of the
Mounted Grenadiers of the Guard

Despite the renown of the Imperial Guard and its prominence in contemporary iconography of the Napoleonic period, there are still many aspects of its dress that are uncertain. This painting of the undress uniform of a Mounted Grenadier trumpeter adds to the controversy by presenting a number of details that differ from those reported in other sources. Perhaps the most startling feature of the picture is the exact shade of dark but vivid sky-blue of the jacket and other parts of the uniform, a point that illustrates the difficulty of reconstructing the look of old uniforms from purely written sources when it comes to matters of colour. The lace on the collar is gold and crimson and not plain gold as shown by most secondary sources, but the Otto artist may perhaps have been over-zealous in depiction of the arrangement of this lace because (1) the vertical line of trim at the back of the collar makes no sartorial sense, there being no seam in that location and (2) there is no similar arrangement of collar lace on any other French Napoleonic uniform. The two-colour trim also appears on the epaulettes without fringe. Rousselot reports that the aiguillette was one-third gold and two-thirds crimson wool, but the mix in this picture appears closer to 50/50.[1] One would expect to find a vertical pocket in the visible coat tail, but none is apparent here. The white cartridge box belt indicates that trumpeters were expected on active service to contribute to the unit's firepower. The belt plate is nearly the same as one illustrated by Fallou, but as usual in Otto paintings the 'flames' bursting from the grenade are not well-defined.[2]

The wearing of a black bearskin cap identical with that worn by Grenadier privates is recorded by a number of sources, but the sky-blue plume shown in this painting is not mentioned elsewhere.[3] The visible portion of the red back patch reveals the existence of orange trim around its circumference, but there is no sign of any other adornment. The sky-blue saddlecloth is also unique, but this departure from the crimson parade model makes for a more felicitous colour combination with the orange trim. The cloak folded on the valise should be sky-blue and crimson by regulation, but the substitution of a trooper's standard white cloak would not have been unprecedented. A trumpeter should theoretically have been mounted on a grey or white horse, but again the difficulties of active service could easily account for the black mount shown here. The arrangement of bridles and saddle straps seems quite accurate.

1 Rousselot Plate No. 45: *Grenadiers à Cheval de la Garde – Trompettes 1804–1815* (Paris 1943/1979).
2 Fallou, p. 197.
3 Fallou, p. 209.

11 and 12
Mounted Grenadier of the Guard
[Front and Back Views]

This pair of pictures provides the last of the three instances in which the Otto artist shows the same subject from two different perspectives, and one can only wish that he had also provided 'rear' views of some of the uniforms in the Manuscript other than those of the Imperial Guard. The fundamental elements of the uniform of this cavalier – bearskin, jacket and breeches – are essentially the same as those of the uniform worn by the Foot Grenadiers, but enough details have been changed to give the Mounted Grenadier a distinctive look.[1]

The two paintings together give a clear view of the straightforward arrangement of the single orange cap cord, which was braided for half its length then narrowed to a single strand ending in the free-floating raquettes. The braided end was anchored near the bottom of the left side of the cap and the middle of the cord was attached to the cap again just above the backpatch, at which juncture a separate tassel was also added.[2] Two unusual points about the head-dress in this painting are that the cap cord ends in two raquettes and there is no cockade below the plume. As in the preceding painting, there is no evidence of a cross of any colour in the circular backpatch, although there does appear to be a ring of orange braid around that space. The chinscales on the bearskin cap are an eminently practical addition for a cavalryman. The moustache and hairstyle of this figure call into question the accepted wisdom that, even on campaign, the

Mounted Grenadiers were clean shaven and wore queues.

The surtout jacket, with its orange counter-epaulettes and an aiguillette on the right shoulder, is quite standard, but there are a number of noteworthy points concerning the equipment of this figure. Rousselot states that the square model of valise with a single orange stripe was not adopted until 1808, at which point a crown had supplanted the grenade as the decoration in the corner of the saddlecloth.[3] The accuracy of the Otto Manuscript is once again demonstrated by the scarlet piping around the outside of the saddlecloth and the distinct detail of the sabre with the grenade ornament clearly visible in the hilt guard.[4] On the other hand, however, the artist was certainly not perfect because the two holster covers seem to have different shapes and the stirrups are incorrectly shown as being triangular. The cartridge box, which might be expected to have had a diamond-shaped plate, here unexpectedly has no ornamentation at all.[5]

As is the case in all pictures of mounted figures in the Manuscript, the complex arrangement of straps, buckles and bits constituting the horse's harness has not been accurately detailed, but the artist has correctly shown the standard, if unwieldy, method by which heavy cavalrymen of the period carried

Continued on page 52

50

11

Grenadier de la
Garde à cheval

11 and 12
Mounted Grenadier of the Guard
[Front and Back Views] *(continued)*

muskets with the butt suspended in a small leather cup and the barrel lashed in close by means of another strap running from the saddle pommel.[6] The musket, like all firearms of the Guard, has brass barrel bands.

The Horse Grenadiers were noted for being mounted on black horses. Hence one finds the following passage relating to the Battle of Austerlitz in the memoirs of Coignet: 'Then the Emperor let loose his "black horses", that is, his horse grenadiers, commanded by General Bessières. They passed by us like a streak of lightning, and fell upon the enemy.'[7]

1 Almost all the features of the service dress of the Mounted Grenadiers shown in this painting are confirmed by a contemporary print by Hendschel of a trooper of the unit in similar attire which is reproduced in Michel Pétard's 'L'Homme de 1807 – Le Grenadier à Cheval de la Garde' in *Uniformes* No. 52 (November/December 1979), pp. 22–27.
2 There is a line drawing of this arrangement in Fallou, p. 205.
3 Rousselot Plate No. 23: *Garde Impériale – Grenadiers à Cheval 1804–1815* (Paris 1966).
4 The photographs of surviving examples of the Horse Grenadier sabre in Michel Pétard's article on 'Le Sabre des Grenadiers à Cheval de la Garde Impériale' in *Tradition* No. 47 (December 1990), pp. 6–10, confirm the accuracy of the Otto artist's work. However, none of the scabbards illustrated in that article and in other sources display the double leather insert shown here.
5 Fallou, p. 209.
6 This detail is shown more clearly in Figure 5–40 in Col. D. Mac-Carthy, *La Cavalerie Française et son Harnachement* (n.l [Paris] n.d. [1985]) (hereinafter 'MacCarthy, *La Cavalerie Française*').
7 Coignet, p. 124.

Grenadier de la Garde
à cheval

13
Trumpeter of the Mounted Chasseurs of the Guard

The noteworthiness of the uniform depicted in this painting depends primarily on whether the lighter colour mixed with crimson in the cords and braiding of this uniform is gold or orange. If it is gold, the painting is merely illustrating (although with a few novelties) the relatively simple sky-blue uniform which had served as full dress during the Consulate but which was relegated to service wear upon the adoption of the lavish hussar uniforms for trumpeters at the start of the Empire. If the colour is orange, however, the Otto artist has depicted a variant of that uniform which is not confirmed by any other source. On the basis of a comparison of the colour in question with the gold of officer distinctions in other paintings and the aurore trim used by the Chasseur private in the following Plate, the case for orange is a strong one.

In either case, the sky-blue waistcoat is unexpected, all other sources being unanimous that this item of apparel would have been crimson with mixed sky-blue braid.[1] Citing unit inventories, Rousselot asserts that the lace on the collar, cuffs and lapels would have been plain gold, but the mixed trim seen here is perhaps not so far-fetched given the prevalence of such variegated braid in the trumpeter's full dress uniform.[2] More difficult to explain is the existence of only a thin line of crimson piping on the outer edge of the lapels and, so it would seem, of the visible coat tail, although this latter feature is frustratingly indistinct. Rousselot agrees, however, that mixed trim would have been used for the trumpet cord, the aiguillette and the Hungarian knots and other decoration on the trumpeter's breeches. The details of the busby are presented in a confusing manner so that the plume, the raquettes and the bag all seem to be on the right side of the head-dress, although the two former items were almost certainly worn on the left. Note the plain piping on the bag in contrast to the variegated colouring of the cords. The cords themselves have been drawn so as to suggest that one of them is draped across the back of the bearskin in the same way that one is draped across the front. No other source, written or pictorial, confirms this detail. As with all illustrations of saddlecloths in the Otto collection, the shape of the item is poorly rendered and all the normal straps and leatherwork have been omitted.[3] This trumpeter is clean-shaven and is mounted on a brown (not white or grey) horse.

1 See, e.g., Fallou, p. 234.
2 Rousselot Plate No. 83: '*Chasseurs à Cheval de la Garde –Trompettes 1800–1815*' (Paris 1963/1981).
3 Compare this with Figure 4 in the colour plates following p. 240 in MacCarthy, *La Cavalerie Française*.

Trompette des Chasseurs
de la
Garde à cheval

14

Mounted Chasseur of the Guard

The Mounted Chasseurs of the Guard were such a favourite unit of Napoleon's and are so well represented in the collections of surviving artefacts from the First Empire, that it is possible to verify almost every uniform detail depicted in this painting against examples of real clothing and equipment. For instance, there is a mannequin of a Guard Chasseur in the French Army Museum in Paris which, except for the fact that it is wearing a bicorne, is dressed identically with this figure from the neck stock to the Hungarian knot decorations on the breeches and the model of sabre.[1] A comparison between the Otto painting and the uniform on the mannequin is eminently favourable to the talents of the Otto artist.

The busby and the saddlecloth are also confirmed by items in the collections of the French Army Museum, but in each case with small but notable discrepancies. In the case of the busby, the surprising items are the cords running across both the front and the back of the cap and the placement of the base of the plume overlapping rather than above the junction of the two. With respect to the saddlecloth, the unusual feature is the bugle horn ornament, which was regulation during the Consular period but which, theoretically at least, had been superseded by an eagle ornament when Napoleon declared himself Emperor.[2] The most logical explanation is that this is an old saddlecloth saved for campaign wear, but in any event the artist has probably drawn the horn backwards and upside down (i.e., it should look like the horn ornamenting the horse's chest strap).

---

1   Willing, Vol. 1, p. 52. The Museum also sells a postcard bearing a colour photograph of this model. The uniform of the Mounted Chasseurs has also been investigated in depth by Rousselot in his double Plate 69–70: *Chasseurs à Cheval de la Garde 1800–1815* (Paris 1966/1980), and Commandant E. L. Bucquoy in a run of eleven sets of his famous uniform cards. The text of these sets, which includes reproductions of many relevant uniform regulations, was later published as a separate volume in 1926 and most recently was reprinted, along with the cards, in E. Bucquoy, *La Garde Impériale – Troupes à Cheval* (Paris 1977) (hereinafter, 'Bucquoy, *La Garde . . . à Cheval*').
2   This replacement process, however, was not completed until the end of 1806. MacCarthy, *La Cavalerie Française*, p. 229.

Chasseur de la Garde
à cheval

15
Mameluke

The Mamelukes were certainly the most exotic soldiers to serve under Napoleon's eagles, and this figure illustrates most of the characteristic features of their dress – the cahouk (brimless low head-dress wrapped with a turban), the yalek (heavy long-sleeved shirt) worn under the short-sleeved beniche (over vest), and, of course, the charoual (massive, loosely-cut trousers).[1] The style of the Mameluke costume (for it was surely that as much as any uniform) was in a state of continual evolution throughout the history of the formation, beginning with the distinctly Turkish/oriental cut of the clothes worn by the first Mamelukes who accompanied Napoleon on his return from Egypt, and with a trend towards a more standardized European look. The dress of the figure depicted here seems right for the 1807 period because the yalek still lacks a collar, but the cahouk is more substantial than earlier versions of the same item and the sleeves of the beniche are relatively modest. There was certainly no standard colour scheme for Mameluke uniforms, but all other contemporary colour illustrations also show crimson trousers.[2] On the whole, however, this uniform is less colourful than those reported by many other sources.

The array of equipment carried by this figure almost perfectly illustrates a contemporary written description of Mameluke armaments: 'Their arms consisted of a short musket ... two pistols in a holster and a sabre similar to that of the hussars, but more curved and worn in a contrary manner (that is to say with the cutting edge of the sabre uppermost, while those of other troops are worn with the cutting edge towards the ground); within easy reach of their hands, they [also] have a long dagger'.[3] As usual, the Otto artist has excelled in detail as with his depiction of the arrangement of the cords from which the sabre is suspended and the exotic fringe decorating the harness. The scarlet saddlecloth is a distinct oddity because every other source shows this item as having been green.[4]

1   Raoul and Jean Brunon, *Les Mamelukes d'Égypte* (Marseilles 1963), pp. 70–73 (hereinafter 'Brunon, *Les Mamelukes*').
2   Because of the novel appearance of these soldiers, they can be found depicted in numerous contemporary works such as a drawing by Zimmerman and a coloured plate by Hendschel. Many of these sources are reproduced or described in Bucquoy, *La Garde . . . à Cheval*, pp. 106–108 and 113–115.
3   Quoted in Brunon, *Les Mamelukes*, p. 74.
4   There is an extensive discussion of the Mameluke harness in MacCarthy, *La Cavalerie Française*, pp. 452–456.

Mameluck.

16
Trumpeter of the Mounted Dragoons of the Guard

The uniform depicted in this painting is one of the most controversial in the Manuscript because it displays a consistent use of white instead of the Guard cavalry's signature colours of aurore, or light orange, and gold for trim and ornaments.[1] In all other known sources concerning the Guard Dragoons, for instance, the epaulettes without fringe are sky-blue with gold edging, the aiguillette is one-third gold and two-thirds sky-blue and the trumpet cord is gold and sky-blue in equal measure.[2] Similarly, the lace on the saddle-cloth and the valise is invariably depicted in other sources as light orange, as is the crown ornament. The trim on the collar has the same peculiar form noted in respect of the depiction of the Mounted Grenadier trumpeter, and the grenades in the turnbacks seem to be white rather than gold.

It seems incredible that the Otto artist could have been so badly mistaken in his colour scheme when, as usual, his command of other details such as the embossed eagle on the leading face of the helmet crest is so expert. One possible explanation is that there may have been a different uniform (using white trim instead of light orange/gold) for the trumpeters of the Vélite squadron of the

Dragoons from that of the regular squadrons, but there is no other evidence to support this theory.[3] Rigo, on the other hand, asserts that this painting represents an undress uniform which was adopted for all trumpeters upon formation of the Dragoons in 1806, and replaced by the uniform with gold appointments only in the winter of 1807/8.[4] He suggests that the white trim is attributable to the fact that the trumpeters of the Line Dragoon regiments which provided the manpower for the new Guard unit all had white lace on their uniform. Perhaps the only point which is certain is that the process of uniforming the Guard Dragoons was lengthy and erratic, so no definitive explanation for this uniform can be proffered. As a final point, it should be noted that this trumpeter, too, lacks the expected white steed.

1   By way of comparison, see the two trumpeters in *surtout* drawn by Rousselot, one in his Plate No. 13: *Garde Impériale Dragons 1806–1813* (Paris 1943/1978) and the other in Plate No. 53: *Garde Impériale Dragons 1806–1814 (II)* (Paris 1979).
2   See, in particular, Martinet Plate No. 230: *Dragons de la Garde Impériale, Trompettes, Grand et petit uniforme.*
3   The Guard Dragoons had a theoretical full strength of 4 regular squadrons and one of vélites, but the final two regular squadrons were not raised until the middle of 1807. Fallou, p. 243.
4   *Le Plumet* Plate No. 217: *Garde Impériale – Dragons Trompettes 1806–1809.*

Trompette des Dragon
de la Garde à cheva

17
Mounted Dragoon of the Guard

In contrast to his trumpeter colleague, this trooper of the Guard Dragoons has a uniform that differs in only a very few details from those shown in contemporary depictions of the single-breasted undress jacket by Hendschel and Weiland. Chief among these is the absence of any coloured piping, which is consistent with Hendschel but not with Weiland, who shows red trim on both the front edge and the collar (and the cuffs also). The knot of horsehair at the peak of the helmet crest (which is in fact simply the knotted end of the decorative 'mane' of the helmet) is separated from the upper tuft by a cylinder of brass, a surprising arrangement given that this feature typically appears either fully enclosed in a brass casing, or porte-aigrette (as depicted by Hendschel and as is the case with all surviving examples of helmets for Guard Dragoon troopers),[1] or completely bereft of ornamentation (as depicted by Weiland and as is the case with some surviving examples of Line Dragoon helmets).[2] The Otto artist may have been observing a campaign modification or an unofficial variant.

The Guard Dragoons were supposed to be armed with the same pattern of sabre as the Horse Grenadiers, which included a grenade ornament placed among the branches of the guard. Nevertheless, the use of a heavy cavalry sabre with plain guard in campaign circumstances would probably not have been unusual.[3] The two sword slings, however, have obviously been incorrectly depicted. They are attached too far down the scabbard to balance the weight of the hilt, and this mistake has further caused the Otto artist to exaggerate the size of the leather inserts in the scabbard's metal frame. Although no musket is in evidence, this Dragoon does sport the regulation bayonet for that weapon.

1   Bertrand Malvaux, 'Les Casques des Dragons de la Garde Impériale de 1806 à 1815', pts. 1 and 2, *Tradition* No. 47 (December 1990), pp. 40–45 and No. 53 (June 1991), pp. 29–32.
2   See, e.g., the Line Dragoons in Plates 73, 74 and 76 below, as well as the photographs of surviving dragoon helmets identified on *Fiches Techniques* Nos. FDr 6 and 8 included with issue number 77 of the French periodical *Uniformes*.
3   See Martinet Plate No. 57, the photograph of a Dragoon/Grenadier sabre on the cover of issue number 47 of *Tradition* and Michel Pétard's article 'L'Homme de 1807 – Le Dragon de la Garde Impériale', *Uniformes* No. 57 (September/October 1980), pp. 26–31.

Dragon de la Garde
à cheval

18
Officer of [Guard] Horse Artillery

Although the attribution of this artillery officer (who, based on his epaulettes and the ornamentation on his breeches, ranked at least as a captain) to the Imperial Guard appears in the caption to this plate only as a pencilled after-thought, his fur busby and golden aiguillette clearly distinguish him from his colleagues in the Horse Artillery of the line. In full dress the Guard's mounted gunners sported a rich blue hussar uniform, but considerations of economy dictated that they wore on campaign this relatively much more modest costume almost identical (except for its colours) with the undress uniform of the Mounted Chasseurs.

The depiction of all the features of the busby has posed an insoluble problem of perspective for the Otto artist, and so his renderings of the ornamental red bag, the gold cords and the chinscales all present physical impossibilities in terms of their positions on the head-dress. In addition, it is surprising to see a busby replete with cording but which lacks both the distinctive Guard Artillery cockade and the red plume which one would expect to see on its left side. On the other hand, the accuracy of this painting in most respects is confirmed by the existence of surviving examples of an officer's jacket and waistcoat which are identical with the jacket and braided red vest depicted here, except that on the museum piece the aiguillette appears on the right not the left shoulder under a modified, and not full, counter-epaulette, an arrangement noted by other contemporary sources.[1] One can only speculate that the reverse arrangement seen by the Otto artist may have been used to mark some now forgotten distinction of rank, between perhaps a Captain and a Second Captain.

The scarlet cartridge box belt with gold button ornaments[2] exemplifies the type of elegant accessory which was de rigueur for a fashionable officer, but the saddlecloth is puzzling because it has the right shape (although poorly drawn by the artist) but wrong colours. According to regulations, an officer's saddlecloth should have had gold edging, instead of red like the rest of the troop, as well as a grenade ornament in the corner.

---

1 The photograph of a mannequin dressed in the full summer off-duty uniform of a Guard Horse Artillery officer appears at page 38 of Willing, Vol. I. See also, Rousselot Plate No. 74: *Artillerie à Cheval de la Garde – Officiers et Trompettes 1800–1815* (Paris n.d.)

2 A similar belt can be seen in the portrait of Captain Montaugon reproduced in Michel Pétard, 'Garde Impériale, 1806 – L'Officier d'artillerie à Cheval', *Tradition* No. 78–79 (July/August 1993), pp. 12–18, at 12.

Officier d'Artillerie à cheval.
de la garde

19
[Guard] Horse Artillery

As with the preceding painting, the busby and aiguillette of this figure identify him as a member of the Imperial Guard, and not of the similarly clothed Line Horse Artillery. Contemporary illustrations of the undress uniform of Guard Horse Artillery gunners (including this one) are so remarkably consistent in detail that it seems certain both that this uniform was meticulously regulated and that the men themselves were allowed little leeway in making those idiosyncratic modifications of their dress so beloved by the true veteran.[1] The identical uniform depicted here is also shown with only microscopic variations by Martinet, Hendschel and Weiland,[2] but there are, as always, a few points worthy of note. First, the Otto artist's skill has deserted him with respect to the busby, so that the plume which was certainly on the left side appears to be growing out of the back of the head-dress. Secondly, the sheepskin saddlecloth (which has been drawn in overly rounded form) confirms that this comfortable piece of equipment, which was used routinely during the Consulate, was kept in service long after it was theoretically replaced by one made of blue cloth.[3] As is the case throughout the Manuscript, the Otto artist here conveys a correct impression of the appearance of the aiguillette, but is not very accurate as to the fine details of the configuration.

1 See Michel Pétard, 'L'Homme de 1807 – Le Canonnier à Cheval de la Garde', *Uniformes* No. 43 (May/June 1978), pp. 21–26.
2 See, e.g., Martinet Plate No. 36: *Garde Impériale – Canonnier à Cheval en petite tenue.*
3 The conclusion is also reached by Rousselot in his Plate No. 60: *Artillerie à Cheval de la Garde 1800–1815* (Paris 1958).

Artillerie à cheval de la garde

20
Elite [Orderly] Gendarme [of the Guard]

Green being the colour favoured by Napoleon for the livery of all his household staff and attendants, it is not surprising to find it predominating in the sombre but elegant uniform of the Gendarme Orderlies. As described by one of them, full dress consisted of: ' ...a green jacket in the style of the mounted Chasseurs with a silver aiguillette and trefoil shoulder-straps, green breeches with lace, [and] a silver-trimmed shako with a white plume; for arms: a partially curved sabre, small carbine and pistol; hussar harness'.[1] The unit's clothing regulations dated 23 October 1806 provide the further detail that the vest was red with silver trim and that the shako had 'a silver plate in the shape of a crowned eagle, silver cords, a black visor, [and] silver chinscales'.[2] The use of silver lace and of black belts trimmed with silver and lined with red cloth by all ranks of the unit provide decisive evidence of the prestige attached to service in the Gendarmes, such items being otherwise worn only by Napoleonic officers. The regulations are absolutely clear that the aiguillette was supposed to be on the right shoulder of each trooper ('*Sur l'épaule gauche un trefle d'argent, sur la droite, une aiguillette de même ...*'), and that placement is confirmed by the miniature portrait of a Gendarme reproduced in the 1911 volume of *Carnet de la Sabretache.*[3] Nevertheless, the left-side aiguillette seen in this painting also appears in Zimmerman Plate No. 18 and Weiland's depiction of a Gendarme, so there may have been different placements used by different companies. The left-side aiguillette is also consistent with the placement of that item in the uniforms of the Guard Chasseurs and Horse Artillery, while the right-side aiguillette is otherwise used only by the Grenadiers and Dragoons of the Guard heavy cavalry. The glimpse of a second belt under the obvious one on the chest of the figure suggests the presence of a firearm on the side of the Gendarme away from view (one belt being for the cartridge box and one for the carbine). The saddlecloth has, as usual, been faultily drawn in terms of its shape and necessary leather straps and reinforcements. The silver lace trim seems unduly narrow and, in this case again, one would expect to find some ornament in the corner.

1   Hippolyte d'Espinchal, *Souvenirs Militaires (1792–1814)* (2 Vols., Paris 1901), Vol. I, p. 109.
2   The text of these regulations is set out in L'Invalide, 'Notes sur les Gendarmes d'Ordonnance 1806–1807' in *La Giberne*, Vol. XI (Paris 1909–1910), pp. 145–152, at 151–152.
3   'Lettres et Notes de Campagne du Général Sigismond du Pouget, Marquis de Nadaillac (1787–1837)', *Carnet de la Sabretache* (Paris 1911), p. 26.

Gens-d'armes d'Élite

21
Mounted Grenadier
[Guides of the Prince of Neufchâtel]

This painting presents the greatest challenge in the entire Manuscript because it depicts a uniform that is entirely unique in the annals of the French Grand Army and which therefore cannot be identified with absolute certainty. On the one hand, the bearskin head-dress of the figure seems appropriate for a member of an élite company of Dragoons, but there is no recorded evidence of white lapels and aiguillettes being worn by any Line Dragoon regiment. The Guard Dragoons, on the other hand, did have white lapels, but they had neither red collars nor bearskins. In the face of this conflicting evidence, in *Le Plumet* Plate No. 174 Rigo links this figure with the Guides of Marshal Berthier, the Prince of Neufchâtel, a formation created on 30 June 1807 from the incorporation of the Guide-Interpreters of the Grand Army (formed 8 May 1807) with the Guide-Interpreters of the Army of England (formed 5 October 1803).

Rigo's attribution, which is not justified explicitly in the text of his plate, has both strengths and weaknesses. Both the constituent units wore green Dragoon jackets (the English Guides with red facings and the German Guides with green lapels and collars but white cuffs) and the latter company also wore a white aiguillette, but there is no surviving information at all about the dress of the combined unit at its inception.[1] Card No. 34 by Victor Huen in Commandant Bucquoy's series on Guides of the General Staff, which purports to be based on a description of the stipulated uniform for the Guides written by Berthier himself on 30 November 1811, shows a uniform identical with that depicted here (although the aiguillette is on the left shoulder).[2] There is also a painting in the Freiberg Manuscript (c.1813) of a similar uniform which has been attributed by experts to the General Headquarters Elite Company, the direct successor formation to Berthier's Guides. Rigo himself, however, has obtained primary evidence that this uniform could equally have been worn in 1807 by the Guides of Marshal Massena.[3] In the final analysis, therefore, the case for this figure representing one of Berthier's Guides cannot be proved beyond some doubt.

---

1 For the uniform of the former, see the decree in Napoleon's *Correspondance*, Vol. 9, pp. 23–24; for that of the latter, see Letter to Marshal Kellerman dated 23 April 1807 in File X(k) 31 at the Historical Service of the French Army at the Château of Vincennes in Paris.
2 Cdt. E.-L. Bucquoy, *Les Uniformes du Premier Empire –Dragons et Guides d'État-Major* (Paris 1980), p. 154.
3 Rigo, 'De Nouveau sur les Guides', *Tradition* No. 16 (May 1988), p. 12.

Grenadier à cheval

PART II
LINE INFANTRY

PART II
LINE INFANTRY

If the Imperial Guard formed the heart of the Grand Army, its backbone was certainly the mass of 'line' infantry, so called because of its role in forming the lines of battle which delineated all major conflicts of the musketry period of warfare. In 1806 and 1807, the full French military establishment contained a total of 89 line regiments numbered from 1 to 112, with 23 of these numbers being vacant (a circumstance which helped to confuse an enemy trying to estimate French strength).[1] All the regiments had three or four battalions, each of which in turn was composed of one company of Grenadiers (with 96 men), one of skirmishers or Voltigeurs (literally, 'vaulters') (with 120 men), and seven of Fusiliers (each with 113 men).[2] The theoretical strength of a complete battalion was 1,042 officers and men, although often no more than half that number of soldiers would actually be present with the Colours in the field.

The basic uniform of French infantrymen had changed in 1793 from the classic white coat of troops serving the Bourbon dynasty to the revolutionary blue jacket first worn by members of the National Guard. As described in the *Etat Militaire de la République Française pour l'Année X*, the full costume was supposed to consist of a blue jacket trimmed with red and lined with white cloth, white lapels trimmed red, red collar and cuffs trimmed white, white vest and breeches, yellow buttons (with the number of the regiment), black bicorne hat and white belts.[3] Grenadiers were customarily distinguished by a bearskin cap and red epaulettes, an imposing combination which drew favourable comment even from their enemies: 'The Enemy's Grenadiers in their Bear-skin Caps, with red feathers, & blue frock coats appeared the most warlike body of Troops possible';[4] 'The red worsted epaulettes give breadth to the shoulders; and the coat, with the facings buttoned back, and the skirts sloped away above the hips, give lightness and height to the whole figure.'[5] The Voltigeurs, which were added to each battalion as a second élite company in 1805, were theoretically entitled only to the distinctions of a chamois, or yellowish buff, collar, but this rule was certainly honoured more in the breach than in the observance.[6]

French uniform regulations of the period encompassed a bewildering variety of prescribed forms of dress (*tenue*), ranging from barracks wear to parade uniform, but one puzzling feature of the Manuscript is that the enlisted men of the line regiments are always wearing a more formal uniform than their officers, even when the two appear in the same painting. The Manuscript thus provides support for the surmise that French officers, despite having the luxury of carrying several changes of clothing in their baggage, may have preferred to wear the pre-eminently utilitarian single-breasted jacket on all but the most formal occasions. This garment placed considerations of economy and serviceability before those of fashion, but even so it was not without a certain grace (or even elegance). This conjecture is also borne out by the lament of one officer of the 15th Line that his expenditure for two new white dress uniform coats was wasted because he 'wore one only three or four times, and the other never'.[7] Another significant point demonstrated by the Manuscript is that officers almost invariably wore the gorget both with full dress and campaign uniforms even though that item of equipment, as a vestigial piece of body armour, had clearly become an anachronism by the start of the Napoleonic period.[8]

Another unusual point about the officers depicted in the Otto Manuscript is that they all seem to be captains. The basic rank distinctions for Napoleonic officers took the form of various combinations of epaulettes, with and without fringe.[9] The combination of a fringed epaulette on the left shoulder and an epaulette without fringe (or counter-epaulette) on the right was, however, used by battalion commanders, captains, lieutenants and second lieutenants alike. The latter two possibilities can be eliminated because they each would have had decorations in the form of coloured lines on the shoulder pieces (i.e., a single red line down the middle for a lieutenant and two for a second lieutenant). In theory the former two ranks could be distinguished on the basis of the quality (i.e., thickness) of the thread used for the fringe (which increased with rank), but such a small difference could easily have escaped the notice of an amateur artist. However, since it seems unlikely that battalion commanders would be appearing with so many individual companies, it is more logical to conclude that the Otto artist was in fact observing captains.

The Otto artist also seems to have had a bias towards depicting Sappers of Line and light infantry regiments since these figures are disproportionately represented in the Manuscript. There were officially only four Sappers for each battalion, all of whom were carried on the strength of the Grenadier company.[10] This bias would be particularly understandable if the splendid Sapper uniforms illustrated in the Manuscript were in fact atypical for units of the Grand Army. There is no definitive way of establishing whether there was in fact a 'normal' uniform for French Line Sappers, but in this regard the Museum of the History of France at Versailles has an intriguing painting by Pierre-Antoine Vafflard (1777–1840?) from the Salon of 1810 which depicts more than 35 French Sappers in 1806 toppling a monument commemorating the Prussian victory of Rossbach in the Seven Years War. The Sappers visible in that work all appear to be wearing standard grenadier uniforms in that they have blue jackets with blue collars, red epaulettes and (to the extent visible) white lapels. Three Sappers are wearing shakos and the rest are wearing bearskins, but all headdresses have red cords and plumes.

Another aspect of French military dress evidenced by the Otto paintings is the use of special unit distinctions to strengthen regimental *esprit de corps* even if, objectively, the expense of such items could not be justified. A letter written by Marshal Soult in May 1808 makes clear both the nature and extent of the problem:[11] 'But there are still many other abuses which merit the attention of the Government both because of the inconvenience they create and the excessive expenses they occasion. All Colonels, both in the infantry and the cavalry, believe themselves to be authorized by custom to make arbitrary changes in the uniforms of drummers, trumpeters and musicians. There are some who, limited only by imagination, pass successively from one style to another and from the bizarre to the ridiculous.' On the evidence of the Manuscript, it seems that this tendency affected Sapper uniforms as well.

During the interval of peace following the Austerlitz campaign, Napoleon promulgated two decrees that were to have a dramatic impact on the look of his army, and the effects of both are well documented in the Otto paintings. Although the light infantry had already been wearing the shako as a regulation item for some time, it was not until 25 February 1806 that Napoleon determined '[w]ith effect from the replacement of equipment in 1807, the shako will be the head-dress of the line infantry'.[12] There were no exact specifications for this new piece of equipment, but it was generally made of black felt reinforced at the top and bottom (often the sides as well) with bands of leather and had a leather visor.

The second decree, dated 25 April 1806, re-introduced white as the basic colour of the French uniform jacket, its use being phased-in through the designation of twenty regiments to receive jackets of the new colour by 1807.[13] The dress regulations relating to the adoption of white uniforms for the French infantry (hereinafter referred to as the 'White Uniform Regulations') put into effect an elaborate scheme for identifying each regiment by means of a unique combination of colours, buttons and pocket design.[14] For this purpose, the 112 line regiments were divided into groups of eight and each group was assigned a distinctive facing colour in accordance with the list shown here.

Within each of these groups, the first four regiments had yellow metal buttons and horizontal pockets, the second four had white metal buttons and vertical pockets. The regiments within each of the quartets were further differentiated as follows: the first regiment had the facing colour on its lapels, collar and cuff; the second, on lapels and cuffs; the third, on lapels and collar; and the fourth on collar and cuffs alone. Any feature left white was to be trimmed in the facing colour.

REGIMENTS		FACING COLOUR
1	– 8	Imperial Green
9	– 16	Black
17	– 24	Scarlet
25	– 32	*Capucine* [Nasturtium Orange][15]
33	– 40	Violet
41	– 48	Sky-Blue
49	– 56	Pink
57	– 64	*Aurore* [Golden Orange]
65	– 72	Dark Blue
73	– 80	*Jonquille* [Bright Yellow]
81	– 88	*Vert-de-Pré* [Meadow Green]
89	– 96	Madder Red
97	– 104	Crimson
105	– 112	Iron Grey

In practice, the distribution of the white uniforms may not have proceeded entirely as planned, since the use of the new clothing can be confirmed for only eleven of the twenty regiments designated to receive it (3rd, 4th, 8th, 14th, 15th, 17th, 18th, 19th, 21st, 22nd and 33rd). In addition, primary sources evidence the use of white uniforms by two other regiments which were not on the original distribution list – the 12th and the 53rd. The re-uniforming process could have some haphazard aspects even for regiments that did receive the white coats, with different companies in the same battalion having jackets of different colours.[16]

The basic motivation behind the white uniform experiment was a desire to reduce the cost of dressing the Grand Army, a cost which had risen significantly as the English blockade made indigo, the key ingredient of the dyes used to make blue cloth, more difficult to obtain and, hence, more expensive. There may also have been political goals implicit in Napoleon's choice of a colour identified so closely with the legitimate royal line of France. In any event, the army, including even that portion of it which had entered military service under the *Ancien Régime*, was never very enthusiastic about the new colour. One officer's reaction is perhaps typical in this regard: 'I was sorry to switch my white coat [for a blue one] in 1793, but I was not pleased to have to start wearing it again in 1806.'[17] In the end, however, it was aesthetics which doomed the project to failure:[18] 'The new uniform was found to be very smart. But that which could impress the Emperor favourably at a military review ... could also horrify him on the battlefield... The appearance of blood on the white coats made even the most trifling wound look serious.' In May 1807 the programme was discontinued for new units, and in the following autumn the regiments that had received the new uniforms were ordered back into blue.

Another relatively new element in French uniforms of 1806–7 was the greatcoat, which had not become an item of official issue until the end of 1805. The Otto Manuscript is nevertheless very consistent in portraying each rank-and-file soldier with such an item rolled on top of his pack, although the colour of the coat generally varies from figure to figure. The most common greatcoat colour in the Manuscript is beige or brown (occurring in eighteen out of a possible thirty-seven cases), while blue coats of one shade or another are found in eleven paintings and grey coats are seen in seven. The memoirs of one anonymous officer of the 14th Light suggest that this type of variety was not uncommon: 'Cloth greatcoats were distributed to the army after Austerlitz, but since most of the cloth was obtained through requisitions made from conquered territories,

one could see coats of all colours in the same unit, which made for a shockingly motley effect.'[19]

1   V. Belhomme, *Histoire de L'Infanterie en France* (5 Vols., Paris 1892–1905), Vol. 4, p. 345.
2   Belhomme, Vol. 4, p. 311.
3   Quoted in Gustave Marchal, *Les Uniformes de L'Armée Française sous le Consulat* (Paris 1901), p. 9 (hereinafter referred to as 'Marchal, *Les Uniformes*').
4   Thomas Henry Browne, *The Napoleonic War Journal of Captain Thomas Henry Browne 1807–1816* (London 1987), p. 229.
5   Moyle Scherer, *Recollections of the Peninsula* (London 1823), p. 182.
6   Decree of the 2nd Complementary Day Year 13 (19 September 1804), *Journal Militaire* for Year 13, Pt. II, pp. 226–228.
7   Toussaint-Jean Trefcon, *Carnet de Campagne du Colonel Trefcon (1793–1815), publié par Andre Levi* (Paris 1914), p. 32 (hereinafter 'Trefcon, *Carnet*').
8   Despite being anachronistic, a gorget could still provide valuable protection. Colonel Trefcon records in his memoirs that he was once struck a blow which would have broken his collarbone had not his gorget attenuated the impact. *Ibid*, p. 82.
9   The various combinations of epaulettes distinguishing the different grades of French officers which were in use during the Napoleonic Period were originally promulgated by regulation of 1 October 1786. E. Cruyplants, *Histoire Illustrée d'une Corps Belge (112eme Demi-Brigade de Ligne)* (Paris 1902), pp. 7–8. They can be found most conveniently illustrated in Rousselot Plate No. 62: *Infanterie de Ligne – Officiers, 1804–1815* (Paris 1958/80).
10 Decree of 7 April 1806 quoted in Alombert, *Le Corps du Mortier*, p. 354, n. 1.
11 Letter of Marshal Soult to the Minister of War quoted in Général Vanson's article 'Les Livrées des Trompettes et Tambours' in *Carnet de la Sabretache* Vol. 1 (1893), pp. 129–138, at 136–137.
12 *Journal Militaire* for 1806, Pt. 1, p. 65.
13 *Journal Militaire* for 1806, Pt. 1, pp. 176–177, and Pt. 2, pp. 14–15. The regiments originally designated to receive the new uniforms were the 3rd, 4th, 8th, 12th, 14th, 15th, 16th, 17th, 18th, 19th, 21st, 22nd, 24th, 25th, 27th, 28th, 32nd, 33rd, 34th and 36th of the Line.
14 Decree of 24 July 1806 in *Journal Militaire* for 1806, Pt. 2, pp. 14–17.
15 See the discussion of this colour in the text to Plate No. 41 (Sapper of the 25th Regiment) below.
16 Colonel Schobert's Order Book, quoted in Rousselot, 'Troupes Françaises', p. 41: '[T]he companies in blue will be on the right, and then will be placed those in white'.
17 Général Bigarré, *Mémoires du Général Bigarré, Aide-de-Camp du Roi Joseph (1775–1813)*(Paris n.d.), pp. 189–190.
18 Beauval, *Souvenirs*, pp. 301–302.
19 Quoted in J. Margerand, 'Infanterie Légère 1806', *La Giberne* Vol. I (1899), pp. 252–256, at 255.

22
Sapper of the 3rd Regiment

Although the existence of Sappers was not officially recognized until early in 1806, such specialist troops were undoubtedly to be found in varying numbers in a majority of units throughout the Napoleonic period, the 3rd Regiment, for example, reporting that in 1804 it needed weapons for sixteen Sappers.[1] As members of the so-called 'Head of the Column' which would lead their unit during any parade or review, Sappers were often dressed in uniforms that owed more to the fashion sense (and purse) of the regimental commander than to any regulation.

This being the case, some variation from the norm might be expected in the dress of any Sapper, but the colour scheme worn by this figure is unique even by Grand Army standards. Nevertheless, a notation in Colonel Laurent Schobert's Order Book for the 3rd Regiment proves once again that the Otto paintings should be believed even when they illustrate uniforms that appear outlandish or inexplicable: '[W]ith effect from September 14, 1806, the musicians will wear a sky-blue jacket with red lapels, collar, cuffs and lining *like that of the sappers* [Author's emphasis].'[2] Except for the colours of the jacket, the dress and accoutrements of this Sapper are relatively standard, although contemporary illustrations of the beige-coloured greatcoats (here rolled on top of the pack) made regulation in 1806 are relatively rare. He wears a new model 1806 shako with brass binding on the visor, but the expected shako plate is absent, having been replaced by a brass grenade ornament. The red shako ornament appears to be a tall, elongated woollen pom-pom rather than a short feather plume, and is a relatively modest decoration for a Sapper. The chinscales have been looped up in a common decorative configuration, with the ends tied together behind the thin piece of lace which keeps the cockade in place. By tradition Sappers were supposed to be bearded, but this figure sports instead a healthy set of side whiskers more evocative of late Victorian than Napoleonic style. Judging from the number of buttons visible on the lower leg, this figure is wearing long gaiters covering the knee, but, as will be seen in other plates, this was not always the case. The poll of the axe appears to be hammer-shaped, an unusual variation.

1   Rousselot Plate No. 89: *Infanterie de Ligne – Têtes de Colonne 1804–1812* (Paris 1965/1981).
2   Quoted in the text to *Le Plumet* Plate No. 208: *Infanterie de Ligne – 3e Régiment, Fifre, Cornet de Voltigeurs, Musicien, Tambour-major et Tambour de Grenadiers 1801.* Rousselot quotes this order somewhat differently in 'Troupes Française', p. 41–42, suggesting that it confirms only the colour of the facings and not the colour of the coats. Neither Rigo nor Rousselot provides information concerning the current location of the original Order Book.

Sappeur du 3.me Regiment.

23
Officer and Grenadier of the 3rd Regiment

A. Officer. The stark contrast between the uniform of this officer and that of the Sapper in the preceding Plate demonstrates vividly that the impracticable and the pragmatic could and did exist side by side in Napoleonic military dress. This painting proves that the blue undress coat was still used by officers even in a regiment such as the 3rd which had received the new white uniforms, probably in an endeavour to avoid both the waste of existing blue coats and the expense of making up new white surtouts (which in any event would not have been as suitable for everyday wear). The detailing of this jacket is relatively elaborate given the red collar and pointed cuffs, piped white, and the red piping on the front and, apparently, on the turnbacks as well, but all these features are noted in Colonel Schobert's Order Book.[1] The other inevitable component of any informal uniform was the bicorne hat, in this case worn en bataille (i.e., the corners aligned parallel to the line of the shoulders). The gold tassels at each corner of the hat were attached to the interior cords used to adjust its fit.

B. Grenadier. The uniform depicted here conforms quite closely to specifications for this unit in the White Uniform Regulations, with three major exceptions: the buttons are silver instead of yellow, the cuffs and cuff-flap are green instead of white, and all green features are piped white. This figure wears the same shako as the Sapper, but without chinscales and trim on the visor. The absence of buttons below the right lapel of this figure is another authentic touch, since Colonel Schobert had eliminated this feature from the uniform of his regiment.[2] His infantry sabre, like many others depicted in the Otto series, has an unusually large pommel on its hilt, although such a feature was in fact present on the pre-1791 model of that item of equipment.[3] Like all infantrymen in the Otto paintings, this Grenadier has a thin brass chain attached to the second button on the right lapel from which was suspended his épinglette, a long, needle-like implement used clear to the touch-hole of the musket.[4] (The tool is not fully visible because it was typically inserted in a button-hole.) According to Colonel Schobert's Order Book,[5] Grenadiers of the 3rd were still wearing their hair in queues during this period.

---

1   Quoted in Rousselot, 'Troupes Françaises', p. 41.
2   Rigo, 'La Tenue de Drap Blanc', *Uniformes* No. 88 (May/June 1985), pp. 19–21, at p. 20, n. 3.
3   Willing, Vol. I, p. 88.
4   A detailed drawing of an *épinglette* can be found in *Manuel d'Infanterie*, plate 4.
5   Quoted in Rousselot, 'Troupes Françaises', p. 41.

Officier et Grenadier du 3me Regiment.

24
Officer and Voltigeur of the 3rd Regiment

A. Officer. This figure is dressed identically with the Officer in the preceding Plate except for the distinctive Voltigeur yellow collar (in this case trimmed red) and the green pom-pom atop his hat. The exact design of the white metal device on the gilt gorget is indistinct, but it is roughly the same shape as the eagle decoration on many surviving gorgets.[1]

B. Voltigeur. This second example of the white uniform confirms that the company distinctions worn with the old blue uniform were preserved intact with the new dress. So one finds a Voltigeur yellow collar in place of the expected green collar, as well as green epaulettes with a yellow crescent (even though the wearing of epaulettes by Voltigeurs was never authorized and, in fact, was expressly prohibited).[2] The green shako cords and the sabre knot with one yellow ring complete the standard package of distinctions for a Voltigeur. As mentioned earlier, the placement of the shako plate just above the visor is a regimental peculiarity noted in Colonel Schobert's Order Book.[3] The plate itself, in the form of an eagle looking to its left mounted on a rectangular base, is unusual for two reasons, although at least one example of a similar pattern of plate exists today in the French Army Museum.[4] The first peculiarity is that the crown over the eagle's head is clearly detached from the plate itself, although this may simply be an error of the artist. The second peculiarity is that the plate gives no indication of the regimental number. The absence of buttons on both cuff flaps is almost certainly an error on the part of the artist, and one that is repeated throughout the Manuscript.[5] Intriguingly, this omission occurs most frequently on the right sleeve of the right-hand figure in paintings presenting two figures.

1   See, e.g., Willing, Vol. II, p. 14.
2   See, e.g., the order of 27 September 1807 prohibiting the use of regimental funds for the purchase of such items. *Journal Militaire* for 1808, Pt. 1, p, 93.
3   See text accompanying Note 21 on page 9 above. Noting that 'the lower leather band [of the shako] is now covered by the pedestal of the Eagle [plate]', the relevant order specifies that the plate will thereafter be mounted above the band. Rousselot, 'Troupes Françaises', p. 41.
4   Blondieau, *Aigles et Shakos*, p. 14, illustration no. 27.
5   Rigo, on the other hand, concludes in his study of this series of paintings that this omission was intentional. See *Le Plumet* Plate No. U5: *Infanterie de Ligne – 3e Régiment, Voltigeurs, Fusiliers et Grenadiers 1807–1808.*

Officier et Voltigeur du 3me Regiment.

25
Drum Major of the 8th Regiment

The splendour of Drum Majors' uniforms is almost an article of faith in the study of Napoleonic military dress, and that faith is justified by the almost operatic lavishness of plumes and gold lace adorning this Column Head of the 8th Regiment.[1] The hat has as much gold lace as, and taller plumes (originally white but they have become discoloured) than, that of a French Marshal. (The cockade may be non-standard since only a large red ring is evident.) The precise colour of the facings of the blue jacket is difficult to determine, seeming as it does to fall somewhere between dark crimson and the evocatively named lie-de-vin ('wine dregs'), and it is buried under a profusion of gold lace. The turnbacks must clearly have been scarlet (to judge from the inside of the coat tail visible between the legs of the figure), as is the piping on the trefoil shoulder ornaments, lapels, cuffs and rank stripes (Drum Majors were the equivalent of Sergeant Majors).[2] The pattern of lace on the collar is worthy of note because it consists of a double line around the top of the collar only and is not continued down the sides of the front opening.

The mace carried by this figure is another Otto masterpiece of detail, from the silver chain wrapped around the shaft to the suggestion of engraving at the neck and the top of the hefty silver knob.[3] The exceptionally sharp silver point to the shaft suggests that the Drum Major may have been able to defend himself with either end of his mace. His more traditional sidearm in the form of a sabre has a silver hilt with a unique four-branch guard and a black scabbard with silver fittings, although gold fittings would be more in keeping with the tone set by the gold lace on the uniform. The sword belt worn over the shoulder is also unique in its asymmetrical arrangement of silver ornaments. Given the de luxe nature of the rest of the uniform, one might expect to find more heavily ornamented boots, but instead we find the model with light brown cuffs worn by almost every other boot-wearer in the Manuscript.

1 This figure is reproduced as Figure No. 4 on Rousselot Plate No. 89: *Infanterie de Ligne – Têtes de Colonne 1804–1812* (Paris 1965/1981).
2 The origins of the office of Drum Major are discussed by Rigo in *Le Plumet* Plate No. 2: *Infanterie de Ligne, 5e Régiment, Tambour Maître.*
3 A photograph of a remarkably similar mace can be found in Willing, Vol. 1, p. 81.

26
Sapper of the 8th Regiment

The bright glamour of the Sapper wearing the new white uniform must have provided a vivid counterpoint to the dark elegance of the Drum Major at the head of the 8th Regiment. In all visible respects (except for its buttons), his jacket fits the description provided by another soldier of the unit: 'When the Regiment receives its new uniform next January [1807], it will be dressed as follows: White jacket, white metal buttons, imperial green cuffs and collar and piping of the facing colour.'[1] The red trimmings of a Grenadier complete an extremely martial picture although the belts are surprisingly bare of traditional Sapper ornaments. There is no cockade on the bearskin cap, but that is true of all the line infantry types wearing bearskins in the Otto series (although it is not true of the figures of the Paris Guard in Plates 67 and 68). This painting also presents the first example of a recurring pattern in the Manuscript in which the decorative cap cords for the Sapper and the Grenadier of a regiment will be the same colour if they are both wearing bearskins. This figure is one of only two Sappers in the Manuscript to have more than one raquette on the right side of the cap.[2]

The gauntlet gloves and apron of this Sapper are clearly non-standard and perhaps represent a capture or acquisition from the enemy. The dark brown colour is the most obvious novelty, but the way in which the apron is worn is itself unusual. In all bar one of the other paintings of Sappers in the Otto Manuscript the jacket seems to be worn over the top of the apron, whereas in this one the top of the apron extends up over the lapels.[3] Moreover, if there is anything holding up the top of the apron it is hidden by the cross-belts because there are no visible apron straps. The axe is much simpler than the others depicted in the Otto paintings, but it still differs from existing examples of the 'regulation' pattern.[4]

---

1 Letter of Charles-Joseph Vanaisse, corporal of the 8th Regiment, dated 22 August 1806, quoted in J. J. Pattyn, 'Deux Lettres d'un Caporal Bruxellois au 8ème Régiment d'Infanterie de Ligne (1803–1807)', *La Figurine* Vol. 42 (Brussels, 4th Trimester 1980), pp. 20–24.
2 There was apparently no official pattern for shako cords during the Napoleonic era despite the prevalence of their use. On the evidence of Otto figures other than the Sappers, the double raquette model of cords was predominant.
3 Rigo omits this feature (and the *épinglette*) in his reproduction of this figure on *Le Plumet* Plate No. 155: *Infanterie de Ligne – Sapeur des 8e, 14e, 18e Régiment 1805–1807*.
4 Willing, Vol. 1, p. 81.

27

Officer and Grenadier of the 8th Regiment

A. Officer. The elegant full dress uniform shown in this illustration demonstrates that the Grenadiers of the line regiments conceded very little in terms of smartness of dress to their brethren in the Imperial Guard. The imposing bearskin cap has a brass plate which appears to have a larger vertical dimension than similar plates illustrated in the Martinet Plate series, and its central device lacks the detailed 'flame' almost invariably found in the stylized renderings of grenades for ornamental purposes during this period.[1] A pragmatic touch is the visor, a detail found in no other contemporary sources (but which is repeated in the painting of the Grenadier of the 95th Regiment later in the Manuscript). The slightly curved sabre worn by the figure appears to have been the type of heavy edged weapon preferred by officers of élite companies for campaign use.[2] The jacket follows the traditional pattern and colour scheme except for the red cuff flaps piped white. One unusual point is the presence of large brass buttons at the edge of the coat below the left as well as the right lapel. There should certainly have been three such buttons on the right side of the coat, but they should have been matched on the left side with three button-holes, thereby creating the theoretical possibility of the jacket being buttoned up across the stomach. The extra buttons in this case may either be a mistake of the Otto artist or an individual modification designed to correct the asymmetry of the traditional 'look' of the uniform. This officer is bare-handed, which is unusual in the Otto Manuscript. The vast majority of all the officers depicted, whether in full or campaign dress, and wearing short white or cream-coloured gloves.

B. Grenadier. This being the first Otto painting showing an officer and soldier from the same company in the same state of dress, it is not surprising to find that this Grenadier wears basically the same uniform as his officer, although it would have been made of coarser materials. All in all, this figure illustrates what is almost an archetypal uniform for French line infantry Grenadiers of the early Empire period with its red epaulettes, sabre with red sword knot and bearskin with plate and red cords. The jacket even has a blue cuff flap with red piping, the colour scheme reputed to have been most common for this feature even though that reputation is not borne out by the Otto paintings. One of the black-and-white drawings by Zimmerman, however, depicts a Grenadier of the 8th with no cuff flaps at all. (This figure also wears overalls and a bicorne hat instead of a bearskin.)

---

1   See, e.g., Martinet Plate No. 16: *Infanterie de Ligne. Grenadier, 58e Régiment (1807)*.
2   Rousselot Plate No. 62: *Infanterie de Ligne – Officiers, 1804–1815* (Paris 1958/1980).

Officier et Grenadier du 8.me Reg:

28
Officer of Voltigeurs of the 8th Regiment

The entire series of paintings relating to the 8th Regiment demonstrates how only a few basic variations in dress can create a rich variety of uniforms within a single unit, and thus this Voltigeur officer looks quite different from the Grenadier officer in the preceding Plate despite the fact that they are wearing the same uniform except for head-dress and colour of the collar. (The lack of buttons on the cuff flap is undoubtedly an error rather than a difference.) This light brown collar is an item of particular interest because this picture (and Plate No. 45 below) may be the only existing first-hand depictions of a Voltigeur wearing a collar in the chamois colour prescribed by regulations. (Chamois was apparently a difficult colour to obtain or to match consistently given the dye technology of the period, so it has been depicted in shades ranging from brown to yellow.) The shako, which seems somewhat taller than should be the case for the 1806 model, is elegantly appointed with a gilt plate and chinscales. The decoration on its upper rim, consisting of interlocking gold circles, is quite unusual for a company level officer of line infantry. Also unusual is the shako plate, which differs from those of the private soldiers depicted elsewhere in the series of paintings covering this unit, but which is the same as that of the Fusilier officer in Plate No. 30 below. This circumstance suggests that there were different standard patterns of plates for the officers and the men.[1] The head-dress ensemble is completed by a majestically tall green plume worn over a green pom-pom.

As in all other relevant Otto paintings, the manner in which the gorget is worn is somewhat mysterious, since there are no signs of either the ribbons which should be running from the ends of the gorget to the buttons securing the shoulderpieces of the epaulettes, or the gold fabric buttons which should be connecting the ribbons to holes in the gorget.[2] The gorgets in the Otto Manuscript also seem to have a wider span than surviving examples, which typically do not cover the full distance from one epaulette to the other.[3]

---

1   The absence of shako cords may be another distinction between officers and other ranks. *Le Plumet* Plate No. U16: *Infanterie de Ligne – 8e régiment, Grenadiers, Voltigeurs et Fusiliers 1807–1808*. See also the discussion of the special regimental pattern of shako plate on page 14 above.
2   Hugo and Malvaux, 'Les Bonnets à Poil', Pt. 2, p. 21, has two photographs of a modern replica of a Napoleonic officer's uniform which clearly show the standard method of wearing a gorget.
3   Compare the gorgets illustrated in the Manuscript with those worn on the infantry uniforms appearing on page 79 of Willing, Vol. 1.

29
[Voltigeur and Fusilier of the] 8th Regiment

A. Voltigeur. The identification of this figure as a Voltigeur is a simple conclusion based on the yellow collar (which is distinctly lighter in shade than the chamois collar of the officer in the preceding Plate), the unique mixed cording of green and yellow on the shako, the green pom-pom, plume and epaulettes, and the green sword knot with yellow accent. The blue cuff flap is noteworthy both because it differs from the red flap of the Voltigeur officer in the preceding Plate and because the painting suggests that the flap has a scalloped, as opposed to straight, edge. Some of the white paint used in this painting has faded, thus eliminating the outer white ring on the cockade and making it difficult to see that the arrangement of belts for the pack is in fact standard. This soldier carries the Model 1777 flintlock musket (with Year IX corrections) which was the standard weapon of all French infantrymen even though Voltigeurs were sometimes armed with a lighter model.[1] The Otto artist is extremely accurate in all his depictions of muskets.

B. Fusilier. This painting has a special interest because it illustrates the black felt bicorne hat which defined the appearance of the average line soldier of the Grand Army prior to 1806. This head-dress was subject to the criticisms that it protected the wearer neither from the natural elements nor from blows to the head, and that it was too easily deformed by exposure to bad weather and hard wear to give a truly uniform and martial appearance to Napoleon's troops. Here the regulation strip of lace holding the cockade in place is orange rather than yellow, the colour called for by regulations.[2] The colour of the pom-pom probably identifies the company to which this Fusilier belonged, but as a standard colour scheme for pom-poms was not approved until 1811, it is impossible to determine which company used yellow during the period represented in the Manuscript. Like any other Fusilier, this figure has plain shoulder-straps instead of fringed epaulettes on his jacket, and only a single equipment belt because Fusiliers were not armed with sabres. A bayonet should have been carried in a scabbard attached to the front of this belt, but none is in evidence here. Fusiliers are supposed to have been clean-shaven, which is certainly not the case here.

---

1 'Instruction sur les armes à feu . . .', *Journal Militaire* for 1806, Pt. 1, pp. 197–240, at 205. Compare the musket in this picture with the photographs in Willing, Vol. 1, p. 87.
2 Specifications of the infantry *chapeau* are set forth in a circular dated 4 *Brumaire* An X [26 October 1801] entitled 'List of the Dimensions and Prices of Items of Clothing and Equipment . . .' (hereinafter the 'Equipment List'). *Journal Militaire* for Year X [1801], Pt. 1, pp. 173–174.

8.me Regiment

30
Officer and Fusilier of the 8th Regiment

A. Officer. This is the sole example in the Otto series of an officer who may have been attached to the staff of his regiment rather than serving with a specific company because his shako sports an ornate gold plume holder in which can be found the white plume characteristic of staff appointments. The shako is otherwise similar to that of the Voltigeur officer in Plate No. 28, but note the additional gold trim outlining the visor and the bottom band. The jacket has a red collar with white trim, and the cuff flaps (at least the right one) appear to have a scalloped edge. (The lack of buttons on the left cuff flap must, again, be a mistake on the part of the artist.) The two lines in the trousers, which are perpendicular to the bottom of the vest, provide one of the clearest examples in the Otto series of the existence of the front 'flap' found in all French Napoleonic breeches. Contrary to regulations, this Fusilier officer sports a moustache. He also wears a pair of the short white gloves favoured by French officers in all states of dress.

B. Fusilier. Given the difficulties of supply in Napoleon's armies, it is not at all surprising to find two different kinds of head-dress being worn by Fusiliers in the 8th Regiment. This figure, presumably a replacement who has recently arrived at the front from the regimental depot, wears a shako with the same distinctive plate as his Voltigeur colleague in Plate No. 29, but in this case it is adorned with a flat, circular white pom-pom. The shako also has cords which were probably plain white in colour, but which now appear to be mixed white and grey due to discoloration. The jacket differs from that of the other 8th Regiment Fusilier in two respects. The first difference is that the button for the shoulder-strap of this figure is placed on the portion of the strap away from the neck.[1] The other difference is that the cuff flap of this figure is red with a scalloped edge. There are, however, two independent errors in the depiction of the latter feature. First, the buttons on the right flap have been omitted. Secondly, the scalloped edge of the left cuff flap should be facing down instead of up. A final Otto touch in this painting is the delineation of the small screw in the butt plate at the bottom of the stock of the musket.

---

1   This variant can be found on at least one Fusilier uniform jacket in the French Army Museum and it is also depicted in a painting by the Bourgeois of Hamburg in a painting of a Fusilier of the 17th Line at roughly this same period. Rigo, 'La Tenue de Drap Blanc', *Uniformes* No. 88 (May/June 1985), pp. 19–21 at 21. This button placement is also depicted in one (see Plate No. 34 (Officer and Fusilier of the 21st Regiment) below), but not the other (see Plate No. 59 ([Grenadier and Fusilier of the] 96th Regiment) below), of the subsequent paintings of Fusiliers in the Manuscript.

Officier et Fusilier du 8me Regiment.

31
Sapper of the 21st Regiment

This column head of the 21st Regiment sports atypical scarlet collar and lapels which once again demonstrates the ingenuity of individual units in matters of dress because these are precisely the facings prescribed for the Regiment by the White Uniform Regulations. In view of the fact that the French Army Museum has white jackets for both an enlisted man and a Sapper of the Regiment, it seems clear that this unit did receive the new uniforms.[1] But what is not clear is whether this figure represents the appearance of the Sappers before the white coat was adopted (which would suggest that the Sappers changed their facings before anything else in the Regiment changed) or after it was discarded (which would suggest that the Sappers retained their scarlet distinctions after the reinstatement of the blue coat). If the latter hypothesis is correct, given the dating of the Otto paintings to the summer of 1807, the 21st must have been very quick to switch back to blue uniforms after the experiment with white uniforms was ended in April.

This Sapper's uniform is completed by a number of typical Grenadier distinctions such as red epaulettes, a sabre and a bearskin with red plume (although in this case the cords are white rather than red), as well as the traditional attributes of his own function – crossed axe badge, gauntlets and white leather apron. His weapon is certainly intended to be some form of short musket or carbine, but the artist has failed completely in his rendering of the weapon's detail. Since the firearm is being carried, the short brass projection above the blanket roll must be the tip of the handle of the Sapper's axe, which would indeed have been carried with its head down strapped into a case positioned exactly where the cartridge box would appear on a rank-and-file soldier, but it is somewhat unexpected to find the handle appearing behind the knapsack rather than between the knapsack and the Sapper's back.[2] The crossed axe badges on the sleeves of the surviving Sapper's white jacket are considerably larger than the ones depicted here, particularly in regard to the length of the handles.

1   These coats are illustrated in Willing, Vol. 1, pp. 57 and 83.
2   Pétard, *Équipements Militaires*, pp. 25–27.

32
Officer and Grenadier of the 21st Regiment

A. Officer. This sombre figure has taken the logic of campaign dress to an extreme to create a form of service uniform in which only the gold buttons, epaulettes and other officer distinctions provide a colour accent. The dark look of the uniform is continued by the black belt with a square gold plate, decorated with an eagle, which supports the scabbard for the curved sabre. There are enough surviving gorgets mounting a silver grenade to indicate that this was a popular pattern for Grenadier officers,[1] but this figure and all the other officers depicted from this regiment are wearing gorgets with an elaborate eagle and wreath ornament which suggests the existence of a regimental pattern for this object. One might expect to see such a utilitarian uniform completed with a bicorne hat, but instead the full dress bearskin is worn. Although the official specifications for Grenadier caps explicitly called for a plate with grenade ornament, this feature was absent at least as often as it was present.[2] Like many other officers, this figure wears a small red ribbon (rather than the full decoration of the Legion of Honour) attached to the jacket by a clasp with two gold arms.[3]

B. Grenadier. If the Grenadier of the 8th Regiment represents the norm for élite company dress, this figure illustrates the details which varied from unit to unit even when bearskin caps were worn: the colour of the bearskin cords, the presence (or absence) of a cap plate and the colour and shape of the cuff flap. The barrel band of the musket just below the bayonet is yellow rather than silver, a feature usually found only on Guard muskets and then usually the other bands are also yellow. A characteristic Otto touch is provided by the depiction of the head of the screw holding the tang of the steel musket barrel to the wood stock. The standard over-the-knee length gaiters are depicted without buttons up the side in all the paintings of the 21st Regiment, but this omission is clearly an oversight which is repeated irregularly throughout the Manuscript.

1   See, e.g., the gorget of a Grenadier officer of the 36th Line Regiment decorated with a grenade device illustrated in Willing, Vol. I, p. 79. Coincidentally, it is displayed on a mannequin dressed in an all-blue *surtout* similar to the one illustrated here.

2   See the description of the Grenadier bearskin in the Equipment List, *Journal Militaire* for Year X (1801), Part 1, p. 175.

3   This type of arrangement is specifically illustrated as a detail on *Le Plumet* Plate No. U13: *Hussards – 5e Régiment 1803–1806 et 1812.*

Officier et Grenadier du 21me Reg:

33
Officer and Voltigeur of the 21st Regiment

A. Officer. This Voltigeur officer strikes the same generally dark sartorial note as his colleague from the Grenadier company, but here the expanse of blue is relieved by a coloured collar which seems closer to buff than yellow in hue, perhaps indicating that officers were more constrained to follow regulations than the men they led. (It is unclear whether the collar has white piping or simply a white stock appearing at its edges.) The waistbelt of green morocco would have been an individual purchase intended to express the wearer's aspirations to the heights of military fashion. The belt clasp, framed by two round bosses decorated with eagles, differs from the standard 'S' shape, and it is hard to imagine a belt design that would call for the green leather to continue under the clasp. The wearing of a bicorne instead of a shako provides further evidence of the popularity of that type of headdress for service wear, but the hat seems barely up to the task of supporting the extraordinarily tall plume. The cloth chin straps for the hat (a utilitarian feature depicted by surprisingly few contemporary sources) are here shown tied up on the right side.

B. Voltigeur. The key point of interest with this figure is provided by the shape of the shako plate, which represents an early version of a pattern that was to be officially adopted by the French Army in 1812, but which was rarely seen prior to 1810.[1] This pattern is characterized by a relatively small eagle perched on a curved base the up-turned corners of which are decorated with lion heads.[2] There are many surviving examples of plates where the number of the unit appears in a central circle on the base of the plate, but none that have the heart-shaped central medallion shown in this painting. The epaulettes of this figure are also unique because of the presence of two coloured crescents above the fringe.[3] The strap for the sabre appears to have two yellow rings, although the second is hard to make out because the colour has faded.

---

1 The 14th regiment of Light Infantry was, however, wearing this type of plate as early as 1805. Willing, Vol. 1, p. 86.
2 See, e.g., Blondieau, *Aigles et Shakos*, p. 40. The early form of the so-called *plaque à soubassement* type of shako plate can be distinguished from the 1812 form by the smaller size of the eagle figure and the fact that the ends of the eagle's perch do not extend outward to connect with the curved tips of the plate.
3 There is a close-up photograph of a pair of Voltigeur epaulettes with double crescent construction in Willing, Vol. 1, p. 83.

Officier et Voltigeur du 21ᵐᵉ Regᵗ

34
Officer and Fusilier of the 21st Regiment

A. Officer. The similarities between the uniform depicted in this painting and those in the two previous Plates serve as a reminder that most regiments had elaborate standing orders concerning the types of dress to be worn at particular times and under particular conditions to ensure a certain uniformity in the appearance of the formation.[1] This figure combines the blue collar and service version of the Legion of Honour worn by Grenadier officers with the hat and green belt (though with a different clasp) of the Voltigeurs. The only novel touch is the blue plume. As might be expected, this Fusilier officer is clean-shaven.

B. Fusilier. The uniform of this Fusilier differs only in minor details from that of the Fusilier depicted in the 1807–8 edition of C.-F. Weiland's series of plates of Napoleonic military uniforms, so it is probably fairly typical of the dress worn by the majority of infantrymen in the Grand Army.[2] The blue pom-pom and plume are almost unique, there being very few examples of blue being used as the identifying colour of a Fusilier company. Once again, there is a button on the outer, as opposed to inner, edge of the shoulder-strap. As in the other Otto paintings of Fusiliers, there is no sign of a bayonet scabbard attached to the single shoulder belt. Although the Otto artist did not excel at portraiture, this clean-shaven soldier looks much more the conscript than the swarthy, moustachioed warriors from the élite companies of the same regiment shown in the preceding Plates.

---

1 See, e.g., Schobert's Order Book. An example of such materials for a cavalry regiment can be found in 'Le Livre d'Ordres d'Un Régiment de Cavalerie (15e Chasseurs à Cheval) Pendant la Guerre d'Espagne 1812–1813' in *Revue de Cavalerie*, Vol. 18, pp. 325–357 (1893–94) and Vol. 19, pp. 28–54 (1894–95).
2 Glasser, *Catalogue*, p. 415. The typical appearance of French Fusiliers is well illustrated in Rousselot Plate No. 3: *Infanterie de Ligne – Fusiliers 1804–1812* (Paris, 1943/1978).

35
Sapper of the 22nd Regiment

The series of paintings relating to the 22nd Regiment demonstrates the danger of assuming that official regulations will be implemented promptly in all their detail, since they provide the spectacle of the Sapper and Voltigeur in variants of the prescribed white uniform while the Grenadier and the officers retain blue coats. As far as can be seen, the arrangement of scarlet facings on the Sapper's jacket conforms to the White Uniform Regulations, because the collar (just visible to the side of the Sapper's beard) is white, the lapels are scarlet (although with white piping, which is not mentioned in the White Uniform Regulations), and the short length of scarlet piping under the right lapel and the glimpse of turnback behind the figure's right leg demonstrate that the turnbacks were white, piped scarlet.[1] The buttons, however, are brass rather than the silver colour called for by the decree, a common variation apparently reflecting a preference for using the regimental buttons of the blue jackets with the new uniforms rather than going to the trouble of having new buttons made. The typical Grenadier distinctions have

been customized to the extent of a white crescent above the fringe of the epaulettes, and the cross belts are richly decorated with brass ornaments which appear to be trimmed red since they are mounted on red cloth.

The apron worn by this figure and those worn by most of the other Sappers depicted in the Manuscript appear to be of the same pattern, which most likely conforms to the specifications for this piece of equipment laid down in a regulation dated 1802 for individuals in the Battalion of Sappers.[2] According to these, the apron was to consist of a four-foot length of leather, narrow at the top and widening to two feet nine inches at the bottom. It was held in place by a strap which passed around the neck and two straps at the waist which tied at the back.

---

[1] This figure is reproduced accurately by Rigo in *Le Plumet* Plate No. 163; *Infanterie de Ligne – Sapeurs des 22e, 45e, 46e, 63e Régiments 1806–1808.*

[2] See the description of an apron in *Manuel d'Infanterie*, p. 81, citing an 'Equipment Decision' dated 11 Fructidor Year X [1801].

36
Officer and Grenadier of the 22nd Regiment

A. Officer. A number of small details combine to make this officer look quite different from the others in campaign uniforms already depicted in the series. The most obvious distinction comes from the decorative cords threaded through the hat, an extreme elaboration on the simple arrangement of cords included in every bicorne of the period to permit adjustment of the shape of that relatively malleable head-dress. It is ironic, however, to find this amount of decoration for a hat used for service wear. The white breeches provide a vivid contrast to the stark blue of the jacket and improve the visibility of the black sword belt. The belt buckle itself is noteworthy because the artist has clearly depicted small right-angled notches in its corners which give it a shape that is truly unique for the period. The eagle devices on the buckle and the gorget are less common than grenades for a Grenadier officer, but the use of these same devices for the Voltigeur officer in the next painting suggest the possibility of a regimental pattern. The officer's sword is straight-bladed, although curved sabres were more common for élite company officers.

B. Grenadier. Although there was no 'official' pattern of plate for the 1806 model of shako, diamond-shaped plates featuring an eagle with spread wings such as the one worn by this Grenadier were probably the most common style.[1] Almost all of these displayed the regimental number, which can barely be seen here under the red cords. The uniform otherwise holds no surprises except for the white crescent surmounting the red fringe on the epaulette and the thin circle of white trim above the tassel on the sabre strap (which is not present on the sabre strap of the regimental Sapper). This painting displays both the strengths and weaknesses of the Otto artist in close proximity to each other – he has forgotten to place the requisite buttons on the right cuff flap, and the bayonet looks quite awkward, but the intricate juncture between the bayonet and the musket barrel is perfectly detailed.[2]

1 Blondieau, *Aigles et Shakos*, pp. 9–11. This is also the style of plate represented in most Martinet Plates of line infantrymen wearing the shako. See, e.g., Martinet Plate No. 4: *Infanterie de Ligne – 88e Régiment*.
2 Compare this detail with the close-up photograph of this juncture in Willing, Vol. 1, p. 88.

Officier et Grenadier du 22.me Reg.

37
Officer and Voltigeur of the 22nd Regiment

A. Officer. This officer is dressed almost identically with his Grenadier colleague, with only the addition of the obligatory yellow collar providing an indication of his company affiliation. The tip of the tall green plume was probably yellow, but the pigment has become discoloured over time. He wears the same black boots with turned-over tops as all other boot-wearing figures in the Manuscript and the expanse of brown leather 'cuff' is, as usual, wider at the front than at the back of the boot although one might expect this feature to have been even all round. Like all Otto Manuscript details, however, this one, although unusual, is worthy of careful consideration. It turns out that the Otto depiction is quite accurate for a style of boot that was extremely popular during this period because it could be used for both mounted and dismounted wear merely by adjusting the tapered cuff. With the cuff turned up, the front of the knee of the wearer was protected against abrasion from a saddle, but the back of the knee was left free to bend without discomfort.[1]

B. Voltigeur. This is surely one of the brightest uniforms in the series, presenting as it does a felicitous colour combination of white, red, yellow and green. As with the regimental Sapper, the details of the White Uniform Regulations have been faithfully observed including, in this instance, a change-over to white metal buttons. The White Uniform Regulations are silent on the subject of cuff-flaps, and the 22nd clearly opted (as did the 3rd) for another chance to display the distinctive scarlet facing colour, which also appears as trim around the yellow collar. The green epaulettes with yellow crescents also appear in Martinet's print depicting this unit (Plate No. 30 Infanterie de Ligne, Chasseur [sic] 22 Régiment), as does the tall green plume with yellow tip, but the figure in that source, dated 1807, is wearing a blue uniform. The shako cords here are unique, however, with yellow instead of green sections supporting the tassels and flounders, as is the sabre knot with its double yellow ring. The greatcoat rolled on the pack is dark medium blue instead of a more typical beige or grey.

---

1 The two forms of this boot are illustrated on *Le Plumet* Plate No. 242: *Tambour-Majors des 16e, 75e de Ligne et 2e Régiment de la Garde de Paris 1807–1808*, the text of which also refers to illustrations of such footwear in the work of Wilhelm von Kobell. Rigo has included visible boot-straps in his paintings, but none in fact appear on any boots in either the Otto Manuscript or the contemporary print discussed in connection with Plate No. 55 (Sapper of the 95th Regiment) below.

Officier et. Voltigeur du 22.me Reg.t

38
Sapper of the 24th Regiment

In theory, the standard French infantry jacket could be buttoned across the stomach using the three buttons to be found below the right lapel, thereby achieving a style similar to that shown by this uniform, but the theory could never be put into practice because the way in which the jackets were tailored did not leave enough extra fabric in the back to permit closure across the front. The jacket of this Sapper therefore represents a true variation in style (including, from the appearance of the visible portion of the turnbacks, short coat tails) which is otherwise unknown in the French army of the period. Infantry of the small kingdom of Württemberg did wear uniforms with such 'half' lapels, but the closure in the front was invariably provided by only two buttons, and the 24th Regiment, forming part of Marshal Augereau's corps, is not recorded as having been stationed in or near Württemberg, so there is no obvious connection to account for the design.[1] The dark sky-blue colour of the collar, lapels and turnbacks is equally inexplicable, it being neither the colour assigned to the regiment for its white uniforms nor one that was historically linked to the regiment by any surviving sources. This uniform may thus simply represent a classic case of a Colonel (in this case Colonel Semelle, wounded at Eylau) dressing his Sappers in whatever manner happened to suit his fancy. Further support for this theory is perhaps to be found in the fact that the Sapper is wearing the short style of gaiter trimmed with red which was normally reserved for the light infantry.

An interesting comparison to this figure is provided by the painting of the side view of a Sapper of the 24th Line which appears in the series of paintings by Zimmerman executed in 1808.[2] This figure wears a bicorne, a single-breasted jacket and long gaiters, and has a sabre with cock's head hilt and a cartridge box worn on a waistbelt, to name only the most obvious differences between the two. Nevertheless, it is intriguing to see that the axes are almost identical, down to the atypical curved hook on the head, and the Zimmerman coat has distinctly short tails. Zimmerman might thus be depicting the campaign dress of the Sapper depicted by Otto.

1 The Württemberg connection is suggested by Rigo in *Le Plumet* Plate No. 239: *Infanterie de Ligne – Sapeurs des 24e, 25e, 30e et 42e Régiments 1806–1810.*
2 Zimmerman Plate No. 5.

39
Officer and Grenadier of the 24th Regiment

A. Officer. With this figure we see once again dramatic results from small variations on consistent themes, because the addition of a second row of buttons to the front of this surtout seems to enhance significantly the martial appearance of the officer. It creates, moreover, a style of dress not duplicated elsewhere in the Grand Army, a military body renowned for its proliferation of styles. Unfortunately it is impossible to tell from this painting how this new style of jacket actually worked because there is no visible opening on the front. (There is, however, a faint indication next to the right-hand row of buttons on the uniform of the Voltigeur officer in the following painting which suggests that the jacket was buttoned on that side.) The uniform is completed by the straight sword worn on a shoulder belt and a bearskin with a single raquette hanging from the right side. The 'flame' of the grenade adorning the plate on the bearskin is better detailed than the previous examples in the series, but still lacks the well-defined tendrils of flame found in most other examples.

B. Grenadier. This is another classic figure which follows regulation quite closely. Note the red cuff-flap, the red cord on the bearskin (with a single raquette) and the exaggerated pommel on the hilt of the sabre. Like all other rank-and-file infantry figures in the Manuscript, this private is wearing black gaiters extending from the top of the shoes to above the knee. The gaiters were secured by a row of brass buttons down the outside of the leg and a leather strap around the leg just below the knee (which is difficult to see in this painting but which is clearly visible in the Plates relating to the 21st Regiment). According to regulations, each soldier was also supposed to own a pair of white gaiters for warm weather dress, but there is little evidence of these being worn by any troops other than the Imperial Guard.[1] This painting also presents a clear view of another Otto detail worth noting; on top of the white leather strap holding the greatcoat to the knapsack can clearly be seen the decorative coiling of the loose end of the strap. Surprisingly, however, this feature, which is prevalent in the preceding paintings of infantrymen, appears only once in the subsequent paintings.

---

1 *Manuel de L'Infanterie*, p. 211. White gaiters were prescribed by the Clothing Regulation of 1786, but were not mentioned in any administrative pronouncements thereafter.

Officier et   Grenadier du 24.me Reg.

40
Officer and Voltigeur of the 24th Regiment

A. Officer. This figure takes the unique dress of his regimental colleague one step farther – by adding a unique head-dress. It is really hard to know what to make of this cap which seems to combine attributes of a shako (such as a precise outline and a tapered shape) with those of a fur busby (such as a bulk larger than a shako and a lack of ornamentation).[1] Based on a comparison with the busbies drawn by the Otto artist for some of his cavalry figures, however, it seems likely that the latter identification is the correct one. The uniqueness of this cap is accented by the unusual two-colour tufted pom-pom at the base of the plume. Other points of interest are the blue piping on the yellow collar, the use of the same eagle ornament as the Grenadier officer on the gorget, and the curved sabre.

B. Voltigeur. The uniform of this soldier is quite an amalgam because he has the same unique pom-pom and plume as his officer, the same style of plate as the Voltigeur of the 3rd Regiment and the same cuff flaps, cords, epaulettes and sabre strap as the Voltigeur of the 22nd. Combined in this case with a blue jacket, however, all these features present a much different appearance from those in the other paintings. This painting also features an atypical number of mistakes by the Otto artist.

First, he has forgotten to colour the portion of the left cuff below the cuff flap (although that omission does create a contrast that provides the best view of a scalloped edge cuff flap to be found in the Manuscript). Next, judging from the portion of scabbard appearing between the legs of the figure, he has portrayed the sabre scabbard as being worn inside rather than outside the coat tails. Finally, the portions of the musket above and below the left arm of the figure appear to have been drawn from different perspectives (i.e., a top view of the barrel has been combined with a side view of the stock). The barrel bands and butt plate of the musket are brass instead white metal, which may mean that this Voltigeur has chosen an artillery musket of the Year IX system which was even shorter than the prescribed Voltigeur model firearm. As is the case for all Voltigeurs illustrated in the Manuscript, the sabre has a noticeable protrusion from its hilt.

---

1 This may be an example of the head-dress which was known as the 'shako à poil', or shako covered with fur, to distinguish it from the busby, which was a head-dress made from fur. See Rigo, 'Les Tribulations du Costume Militaire: Les Hussards – Deuxième Époque, La République et le Consulat', *Uniformes* No. 33 (September/October 1976), pp. 6–16, at 15 (hereinafter referred to as Rigo, 'Hussards, 2e Époque').

41
Sapper of the 25th Regiment

There are no modern definitions or descriptions of the colour '*capucine*' which was assigned to the 25th Regiment for the facings of its white uniforms,[1] but some clue as to its appearance is perhaps provided by the fact that it is the French name for the flower known as nasturtium in English, which is typically orange in colour. If the orange facings in this painting represent that colour, this Sapper provides another example of one of the regiments designated to receive the white uniform using the distinctive colour but not the white uniform itself. The only detail inconsistent with this analysis is the fact that the 24th Mounted Chasseurs, which also had *capucine* as its distinctive colour, is depicted later in this series with facings of a much deeper red orange than the colour appearing here. This Sapper is wearing a Grenadier-style bearskin with red cords, but the single tassel which in other instances is found at the top of the front of the head-dress is seen here behind the plume. The crossed axe badges on the sleeve of the Sapper seem to be in the facing colour rather than red, but in contrast the glimpse of the turnbacks visible behind the apron shows that this feature was red instead of white, as is the decorative trim on the short gaiters. The cuff flap on the left sleeve has been drawn upside down.

As for the equipment of the figure, it is unusual to find an ornament on the sword belt without one on the belt for the axe case. Even more peculiar is the fact that both the sword belt and the sabre are identical with those carried by the Sapper of the 85th (see Plate No. 50 below) down to the red trim under the brass grenade and the short projection from the hilt of the sword. The majority of line infantry Sappers in the Manuscript (eight, to be exact) are carrying firearms that have a long length of barrel visible beyond the end of the wooden stock and of the ramrod, a configuration which is present in both the Hussar and Gendarme model carbines in the Year IX system.[2] The musket of this figure, however, has both a brass band and its ramrod visible quite close to the muzzle, neither of which features is readily explicable. The axe has a compact shape which would make it better suited for handling than many of the others depicted in the Otto series. This figure has only a moustache instead of a beard.

---

1   English language texts describing the White Uniform Regulations are unhelpful in this regard because they tend to use the French word without translation. See, e.g., Emir Bukhari, *French Napoleonic Line Infantry* (London 1973), p. 61.
2   Dominique Venner, *Les Armes à Feu Françaises* (n.l. [Spain] 1979), pp. 284–285.

Sappeur du 25.me Regiment.

42
Sapper of the 45th Regiment

Given the colour schemes displayed by the preceding Sapper uniforms in the Manuscript, it is not difficult to guess on the basis of this painting that the 45th Line Regiment was assigned sky-blue facings by the White Uniform Regulations. What is more surprising is the fact that the 45th Regiment was not one of the units designated to receive the new uniform and, indeed, there is no evidence that such dress was ever issued to that regiment. Thus, on the evidence of this and other paintings in the Otto series, it seems that some units used the excuse of the white uniform scheme to devise a more distinctive style of dress to emphasize their respective distinctive identities. A further novelty is the fact that both the collar and lapels appear to have dark blue piping, which may also have been the case with the turnbacks because there is no piping of another colour evident on the edge of the jacket below the lapels where the piping for the turnbacks should begin.

The uniform of this Sapper, however, is noteworthy for many reasons other than the colour of its facings. The bearskin is to be expected, but in this case the cording consists only of a single raquette suspended from the left side. The sleeve badge provides another Otto treat; this obligatory symbol of function has here been transformed into a minor artistic masterpiece. The figure is wearing blue breeches with his short gaiters with red trim, and there even appears to be a red stripe down the outside of the gaiter under the buttons. The equipment is also elaborate and unusual. The appearance of the cross-belts is somewhat mysterious, because the location of the two narrow tongues inside the square buckle on the Sapper's breast would logically suggest that the buckle belongs to the sabre belt, but the brass-tipped projection of belt on the other side would seem to suggest the contrary. In any event, the six-pointed stars on the sword belt and the crossed axe over grenade ornament on the left shoulder belt reflect a de luxe attention to detail. The sword itself is highly unusual both in terms of its size and design, with the hilt featuring an odd-shaped pommel.[1] The axe, with that slender, murderous-looking spike projecting from the top of the handle, also seems to be the product of especially careful craftsmanship. The two-colour gauntlets may either have been another regimental oddity or a conceit of the individual Sapper. This painting also provides the second example in the series of a Sapper with bushy sideburns rather than a full beard.

---

1   Rigo has rendered the pommel as a bird in *Le Plumet* No. 163, but that conjecture seems wide of the mark.

43
Grenadier and Drum Major
of the 45th Regiment

A. Grenadier. This figure illustrates the rarest form of adaptation of the white uniform facing colour by a line unit – its use as a replacement for the traditional red colour of the collar and cuffs of the uniform of a Grenadier private. And, as sometimes one good novelty will beget another, these different colour facings are piped with white, even though the cuff flap (in this case blue) retains the more traditional red piping. The rest of the uniform follows a more traditional pattern, except that the shako anticipates by some years the Grenadier practice of having the reinforcing bands of the head-dress coloured red. The standard Charleville musket Model 1777 (corrected Year IX) carried by this figure is beautifully rendered by the Otto artist, but like most others in the Manuscript, it seems to lack the prescribed white sling.[1] The bayonet, however, seems unusually short, a problem also present in many other paintings.

B. Drum Major. The uniform of this figure follows quite closely the style of uniform worn by the Drum Major of the 8th Regiment depicted in Plate No. 25, a coincidence which suggests the existence of certain stylistic norms for individuals of this rank, but this Drum Major is by far the more lavishly dressed of the two. The most significant difference is most undoubtedly the imposing fur busby set off by the dark sky-blue ornamental bag with gold trim, the gold chinscales and the tall blue plume resting on a base arrangement of red ostrich feathers. The gold trim on the jacket is generally the same except that the three buttons under the right lapel and the corresponding three button-holes under the left lapel have been picked out with individual lengths of lace. The trefoil shoulder-straps are blue trimmed gold instead of entirely gold, and there is a hint of a cuff flap on the left sleeve. The white vest is cut straight across the bottom and lacks visible pockets, and both it and the white breeches are elaborately decorated with gold filigree. The Drum Major appears to be wearing boots trimmed across the top with gold. His mace is almost identical with that of the 8th Regiment Drum Major, but his silver hilted sabre has only a single branch guard.

---

1   Compare this painting with the sling illustrated in Martinet Plate No. 214: *Garde Impériale – Grenadier 3e Régiment* and the photograph in Willing, Vol. I, p. 87.

Grenad: du 45.me Reg: Tambour major.

44
Sapper of the 46th Regiment

The great challenge in studying the Otto Manuscript is that of looking past the similar poses, styles and colours to pick out the subtle details that give these paintings so much of their value. With this figure, one starts with the sky-blue facings which, preliminarily at least, would appear to be inspired by the White Uniform Regulations just as were the facings of the Sapper of the 45th Regiment. But it is obvious that the shade of these facings is quite different from that of the latter, and in fact appear to be the same colour (and share the same red piping) as those of the Sapper of the 24th Regiment. (They are also similar to, but darker than, the facings on the Sapper of the 94th Regiment.) These points, as well as the fact that the facing colour is arranged in a manner inconsistent with the White Uniform Regulations because it also appears on the collar (judging from the small patch visible next to the right side of the figure's beard), suggest that the method of distinguishing the Sapper's uniform derives in this case from a source other than the white uniform colour scheme. Unfortunately we possess no information as to what that source might have been.

The next detail of this figure that seems odd is the intersection of the cross-belts on the Sapper's chest. This diamond-shaped area does not appear to belong to either belt, which raises the possibility that the Otto artist simply forgot to draw in a belt plate or a belt buckle, either of which would provide a more understandable explanation for the space in question. The figure also lacks a visible sling for the musket (which seems to be of the same atypical model carried by the Sapper of the 25th Regiment in Plate No. 41 above). The purpose of the small pouch or bottle slung over the Sapper's left shoulder is probably personal rather than professional, and its presence in this painting is noteworthy because it highlights the lack of unofficial accoutrements in all the other paintings in the Manuscript despite the common campaign use of such equipment by Napoleonic soldiers.[1] The final surprising detail in the dress of this figure is the blue tip to the red plume, which is veritably unique among the known variations of Sapper distinctions.

---

1 In *Le Plumet* Plate No. 163: *Infanterie de Ligne – Sapeurs des 22e, 45e, 46e, 63e Régiments 1806–1808*, Rigo identifies this pouch as a powder flask, but that identification seems unjustified.

45
Officer and Voltigeur of the 46th Regiment

A. Officer. This figure presents the odd combination of a simple campaign jacket with an elaborate full dress shako which seems to fit nearly perfectly the description of the 'super fine' model of shako advertised in September 1807 by a Parisian manufacturer of military equipment: 'trimmed with gold lace 18 lines in width at the top, 15 lines in width at the bottom, also gold chevrons 8 lines in width; visor bordered with gilded copper'.[1] The only other primary sources that show such chevron decorations with the point facing up, as opposed to down, are Plate No. 51 (Officer and Grenadier of the 85th Regiment) below and Martinet Plate No. 201: Officier d'Infanterie de Ligne. The advertising circular noted above makes it clear that chinscales, cords, plumes and pompoms all had to be purchased separately, so the officer here has not spared any expense. The boss connecting the chinscales to the shako is decorated with a face, but at this scale it is impossible to tell whether it represents the head of Medusa or of a lion, the two most popular motifs. The shape of the shako plate is less distinct than that worn by the other figure in this painting, and it does not resemble closely any other known examples of the plate with the stylized crescent base that eventually became regulation in 1812. It is odd that this Voltigeur officer has a different colour pompom from the Voltigeur private to his left. The rest of the uniform is relatively unremarkable except that the collar of the coat appears to be brown/beige rather than yellow, providing another example of the use of the chamois colour prescribed by regulation but rarely worn in practice. There is a suggestion of blue piping at the opening of the collar, but this dark colour may simply be shading.

B. Voltigeur. This soldier's dress and equipment is almost identical with that of the Voltigeur of the 24th Regiment illustrated in Plate No. 40, down to the musket with brass trim, and only the following differences being apparent: red tip to plume, green pom-pom and red instead of yellow trim on the green sword knot. This figure also has a green cord slung across his chest which may have been attached to a canteen or to a bugle horn of the type used by Voltigeur units instead of drums for signalling.[2] This soldier's cockade is also unusual, because it differs from that of his officer and most of the other figures in the Manuscript in having a red ring surrounding a blue centre and no white ring at all.

1   Quoted in Henri Depontaine, 'Ce Qu'on Apprend par de Vieux Prospectus 1807–1813', *Le Passepoil* Vol. 3, No. 2, pp. 25–31.
2   'In place of drums, this [Voltigeur] company will have as military instruments small hunting horns called *cornets*.' Napoleon I, *Correspondance*, Vol. 9, p. 287.

Officier et Voltigeur du 46.me Reg.

46
Sapper of the 54th Regiment

The exact shade of the red facings worn by this figure is somewhat difficult to identify because it seems to be a different colour from both the dark red of the epaulettes and the scarlet red of the plume on the bearskin. The White Uniform Regulations are no help in this instance, because they prescribed pink facings for the 54th, but a look back into the history of the Regiment provides another possibility. The 54th Regiment of the First Empire was the lineal descendant of the Royal Roussillon Regiment, and under the 1791 and 1792 dress regulations, that regiment wore a white uniform faced with crimson.[1] It does not seem too far-fetched to hypothesize that in a search for distinctive dress, this regiment may have tried to revive an old regimental distinction, but this does not explain the blue piping on the lapels and collar.

The bearskin and cords of this Sapper are identical in style with those of the Sapper of the 45th, but the axe badge on his arm (which appears to be the same colour as the gauntlet gloves, edged in red) is unique. Unique, too, is the unidentifiable animal figure-head forming the pommel of the sabre. The glimpse of leg just to the left of the apron shows that this uniform was completed by blue breeches worn with short gaiters trimmed red at the top. The uncomplicated, single-bladed axe is the one in the Manuscript that perhaps comes closest to looking like the axe prescribed by regulation.

1 Michel Pétard, 'L'Infanterie de 1791: Le Fusilier de la Ligne', *Tradition* No. 36 (January 1990), pp. 10–20 and No. 37 (February 1990), pp. 40–42.

47
Sapper of the 63rd Regiment

The French colour aurore is another shade that defies exact definition, although the fact that its name is also the French word for 'dawn' strongly suggests a colour in the orange/yellow range. Given that circumstance, the reference to aurore facings in Lieutenant Beauval's Souvenirs, and the assignment of aurore to the 63rd Regiment in the White Uniform Regulations, it seems logical to conclude that the orange shade displayed on the collar and lapels of this figure is in fact that colour.[1] Coincidentally, a similar shade of facings for Sappers and Musicians of the 63rd is also illustrated in the Bucquoy series in paintings based on figures in one of the collections of Alsatian paper soldiers.[2] The blue lines surrounding the collar suggest that both the collar and lapels had blue piping, but this is difficult to verify on the sides of the lapels. The most obviously striking feature of the dress of this figure is the substitution of a fur busby for the almost invariable Grenadier-style bearskin head-dress, a regimental distinction also shown in Zimmerman's drawing of a Sapper of the 63rd. Several commentators have concluded that the slightly odd shape of the lower edge of the busby is caused by a leather visor to the cap, but even on close scrutiny no such feature is distinctly discernible in the original painting.[3] The single strand of white cord supports two raquettes, instead of the usual one, and the typical red plume in this instance sits on top of a spherical red pom-pom. The light brown apron worn over the jacket is also atypical, as are the two-colour gauntlets. Even more unusual, however, are the details revealed by the glimpse of leg visible next to the apron: blue breeches with a thick, scallop-edged orange stripe and short gaiters with red trim and a red tassel at the top (all of which are confirmed as to form, but not colour, by Zimmerman). Lest one assume that Sappers had a purely ceremonial function, Beauval relates that at the 1809 Battle of Medellin, the Sappers of the 63rd led an assault 'using their axes like Mamelukes use their scimitars, lopping off heads at a single blow'.[4]

1 On the other hand, all the Martinet Plates showing units with *aurore* facings show a distinctly lighter shade of orange. See, e.g., Martinet Plate No. 138: *Officier de Dragons – 25e Régiment*.
2 E.-L. Bucquoy, *Les Uniformes du Premier Empire: L'Infanterie de Ligne et L'Infanterie Légère* (Paris 1979), p. 170, citing as a source paintings by 'Piton', presumably a reference to Fr. Piton (1790–1874), the historian of Strasbourg. Francois Lotz, *Les Petits Soldats d'Alsace* (Strasbourg n.d.), p. 68.
3 See, e.g., *Le Plumet* Plate No. 163.
4 Beauval, *Souvenirs*, p. 302.

48
Officer and Grenadier of the 63rd Regiment

A. Officer. As discussed in the the first section of this book, the jacket shown in this painting illustrates exactly the surtout described by Lieutenant Beauval of the 63rd in his memoirs, and so provides one of the strongest pieces of evidence concerning the authenticity of the Manuscript. The painting also makes it clear that the aurore piping extended to the outline of the blue turnbacks and to the pointed cuffs, although that on the left sleeve has now become so badly discoloured as to be almost unrecognizable. Colonel Mouton-Duvernet's predilection for fancy dress is also evident from the shako worn by this officer. The shape is regulation, but the gold trim consists of a double stripe around the base and another line of lace delineating the edges and centre seam of the shako visor. The shako plate in the form of a grenade with the regimental number inscribed on the hemispherical base is unusual, but not unique, for a similar device is illustrated by Richard Knötel on the bearskin of a Grenadier of the 117th Regiment from a later date.[1] Most commentators have concluded that the dark portion of the plume is a white base which has become discoloured,[2] but the discoloration might equally well be obscuring a gilt plume holder with a vandyked upper edge, although it would be odd to find such a holder starting above rather than below the red pom-pom.

B. Grenadier. This soldier wears a shako similar in shape and style to that of his officer, but with distinctive thick red trim on all the supporting leatherwork. Such trim on the headdress of élite company personnel (red for Grenadiers, yellow for Voltigeurs) only gained official recognition in the 1812 uniform regulations, but it certainly was widely applied, particularly after the use of distinctive shako cords and plumes was abolished in 1810.[3] This shako differs from later examples in that there are only two (and not four) angled bands of trim forming the chevron on its side. The shoulderstrap of the epaulette on this figure's left shoulder is blue with red trim, but because of the way the other epaulette has been drawn it is difficult to come to a decisive conclusion as to whether or not this is another error on the part of the artist. The detailing on the gaiters is generally weak throughout the Manuscript, but in this Otto painting there is for once a depiction of the brass buckle on the supporting strap below the wearer's knee.

1   R. Knötel, *Uniformenkunde* Vol. 16, plate no. 35.
2   See, e.g., Rousselot Plate No. 17: *Infanterie de Ligne –Grenadiers et Voltigeurs 1804–1813* (Paris 1943/1978).
3   A close-up view of this type of trim is provided by the colour photograph of the 1812 Model shako of a Grenadier of the 88th Line Regiment which appears on page 54 of Blondieau's *Aigles et Shakos.*

Officier et Grenadier du 63.me Regiment.

49
Drum Major of the 75th Regiment

This figure, the sole representative of his regiment in the Manuscript, is the only one in the Manuscript that must be identified exclusively on the basis of the written caption, there being no other evidence to connect this Drum Major with the 75th Line. He is dressed less ostentatiously than his colleagues in the 8th and 45th Regiments, and the absence of plumes on his hat combined with the wearing of a plain white waistcoat indicate that he is wearing an undress variant of his full uniform. The combination of colours and gold trim is none the less striking.

The gold cords used to hold the hat in shape have taken on a decorative role and are even thicker than (although not so numerous as) those on the hats of the officers of the 22nd Regiment in Plates 36 and 37. The scarlet jacket has pointed cuffs and pointed lapels, both of which features are more typical of Light rather than Line infantry uniforms, and it also has scarlet turnbacks. Given the richness of the jacket, it seems almost anticlimactic that there is no gold lace for the button-holes of the lapels or the white vest. The unusual blue breeches with intricate gold Hungarian knot decorations complete the outfit. The green leather sword-belt would have been the height of fashion, and it supports a very elegant-looking sabre. The silver head of this figure's baton has a flat top.

According to Rigo, the name of the Drum Major of the 75th Regiment of the Line during the period from 1804 to 1809 was Jacques Ledraps (born 1779).[1]

---

1 *Le Plumet* Plate No. 242: *Infanterie – Tambours-Majors des 16e et 75e de Ligne et du 2e Régiment de la Garde de Paris.*

Tambour major du 75.me Regiment.

50
Sapper of 85th Regiment

The classic eagle of Napoleonic iconography and heraldry, as typified by the model of eagle used for the standards of the French Army (and as almost invariably depicted in the Otto Manuscript), is a perching bird with wings deployed in a very stiff and unnatural fashion to expose its breast. On the shako plate of this Sapper, however, appears a significantly different creature, its wings uplifted as if the eagle were about to take flight.[1] This variant was far from common and the fact that the Otto artist was able to distinguish its appearance from the norm once again provides proof of the painstaking care taken in the Manuscript to depict uniform details in an accurate way. The shako itself is standard, although it has been drawn in such a way that the reinforcing bands of black leather are easier to discern here than in most of the other paintings. The red spherical pom-pom with tuft is unique for the Manuscript.

Head-dress aside, the uniform worn by this figure bears an astonishing resemblance to that worn by the Sapper of the 21st Regiment which appears in Plate No. 31 above, the only difference being the presence of brass ornaments on the belting. (The wearing of the top of the apron over rather than under the jacket does not seem to represent a true sartorial distinction.) The similarity is complete down to the splash of red next to the Sapper's apron which may be either be a portion of a red coat tail or, more radically, of red breeches (although, given that the gaiters appear to be full length, the former possibility seems to be the more likely one). There is no obvious reason for this coincidence, but it is intriguing to find that both regiments formed part of General Charles-Etienne Gudin de la Sablonnière's division of Marshal Davout's Third Corps. The firearm carried by this Sapper is unique in the Manuscript, considerable lengths of both barrel and ramrod being visible, without a sign of the stock. This configuration is consistent with the appearance of Year IX model cavalry carbines.[2]

---

1 The photograph of a surviving shako plate which could have been a model for the one shown in this painting appears in Blondieau, *Aigles et Shakos*, p. 16. The resemblance is all the more uncanny because that plate bears the number '58' as opposed to the number '85' on the plate in the painting.
2 Laurent Mirouze, 'Le Mousqueton de Cavalerie An IX', *Tradition* No. 12 (Jan. 1988), pp. 37–41, and No. 14 (March 1988), pp. 28–32.

51
Officer and Grenadier of the 85th Regiment

A. Officer. As mentioned in connection with Plate No. 45 above, the inverted golden chevrons on the side of the shako of this officer is a style of decoration relatively rare in the annals of French Napoleonic dress.[1] While there is thus some precedent for this shape of the chevrons on an infantry shako, there is less for the number of chevrons.[2] Nevertheless, it seems that three chevrons was the standard for distinguishing the cuffs of Hussar captains.[3] The other curious point about the dress of this officer is the absence of any colour except blue, a circumstance found elsewhere only in the uniforms of the officers of the 21st Line. This unusual similarity in dress between these two regiments from the same division provides further basis for speculation about the existence of divisional standards of dress.

B. Grenadier. If all the uniforms in the Otto Manuscript were unique, it would probably be more difficult to find them all believable, so the occasional appearance of a soldier dressed substantially in accordance with 'regulations' is a welcome sight. The only non-standard item in the uniform of this Grenadier is the red (rather than blue) cuff flap, although the evidence of the Manuscript suggests that this variation was in fact worn more often than the standard itself. Both cuff flaps have scalloped edges, and the one on the right sleeve has probably been drawn upside down. The musket shares the same unusual brass muzzle band as that of the soldier in Plate No. 32 above.

---

1 Another example is illustrated in Rousselot Plate No. 52: *Artillerie à Cheval – Officiers et Trompettes, 1804–1815* (Paris 1943/1979), albeit without supporting citations. This style of shako chevron also seems to have been used in the Westphalian army based on the evidence of Weiland's print of a Westphalian Horse Artillery Officer and of two paintings of Westphalians from the so-called 'Frankfurt Collection', one of a foot artillery officer and the other of an officer of light infantry, reproduced in black and white plates of the *Vincit* series drawn by R. Marrion for Norman Newton Ltd. in the early 1960s.

2 There is another contemporary illustration of a Grenadier officer with numerous inverted chevrons on his shako to be found in the sketchbooks of Charles Hamilton Smith, a British officer and artist famous for his work on the costumes of the British Army, but there are so many peculiarities about the uniform worn by the figure portrayed in the painting, who was probably a prisoner of war from Haiti, that no realistic conclusions can be drawn from this precedent. (The Smith sketchbooks are in the Victoria and Albert Museum in London.)

3 Rousselot Plate No. 54: *Hussards – Officiers 1804–1815* (Paris 1979).

Officier et Grenadier du 85.ᵐᵉ Regiment.

52
Officer and Voltigeur of the 85th Regiment

A. Officer. The addition of a yellow collar trimmed red clearly differentiates this officer from his Grenadier colleague, as does the unusually elongated green pom-pom with red tuft. The wide style of waistbelt worn by both officers is atypical, especially considering the position of the second strap holding the frog for the sabre scabbard and the absence of any belt plate. Also unusual is the brass fitting in the middle of the sabre scabbard.

B. Voltigeur. As usual with any Otto figure, close scrutiny pays great dividends in identification of unusual uniform features. For instance, the red, white and blue cockade on this shako features a disposition of the colours that reverses the normal pattern for the two outer rings, a characteristic it shares with only two other French cockades in the Manuscript.[1] Next, the epaulettes have a triple layer of cres-

cents at the end of the shoulder piece.[2] Finally, the sabre has the same unusual projection at the tip of the pommel found in several other paintings of Voltigeurs. The musket appears to have a steel middle band between upper and lower brass bands, a configuration found only on the Dragoon-pattern musket of the Year IX system.

1 Of the sixty-one other cockades in the Manuscript, fifty-nine are coloured (reading from the outside ring to the centre) white, red and blue, one is coloured red, blue and white and one is coloured just red and blue. By way of comparison, in the Manuscript of the Bourgeois of Hambourg, forty-eight of the seventy-six cockades illustrated have the popular white, red and blue disposition of colours, while twenty-three are red, white and blue like that of this Voltigeur. Three others are coloured blue/white/red, and two feature the sequence blue/red/white. F. Buttner, 'La Compagnie de Reserve du Dèpartement des Bouches de L'Elbe 1811–1814', *Carnet de la Sabretache* No. 19 (1973), pp. 97–102, at p. 102.

2 There are no surviving examples of an epaulette with that feature, but one with a double crescent is shown in Blondieau, *Aigles et Shakos*, p. 83.

Officier et Voltigeur du 85.me Regiment.

53
Sapper of the 94th Regiment

The uniform of this Sapper is quite similar to that of his counterpart in the 46th Regiment shown in Plate No. 48 above, but a number of small differences make for a noticeably different ensemble. The most significant of these are red cords on the bearskin and a lighter shade of medium blue for the lapels, and there is also a profusion of brass buckles and ornaments on the crossbelts. The ornaments lack precise detail, but the faces are suggestive of the type of stylized lion head boss that can be seen today on artefacts in the French Army Museum[1] and which is clearly depicted on the Sapper belting illustrated in Plate No. 2 (Sapper of the Imperial Guard). The rest of the equipment is also of interest: the axe has an unusual ring of brass just below the head, and the sidearm seems to be a variant of the cock's

head hilted sabre-saw which was supposed to be regulation for Sappers but which, on the evidence of the Manuscript at least, was not often worn. The features of the sword which define the variation are partial striations on the hilt, the red sword knot and the fact that the ends of the hilt guard curl in different directions. The long silver pipe arising behind the left shoulder of the Sapper is undoubtedly an attempt by the Otto artist to draw the Sapper's musket, but the depiction is incomplete because there is no strap to hold the weapon in place. A small glimpse of cloth just off the left side of the apron confirms that the uniform was completed by white breeches worn with short, red-trimmed gaiters.

1   Willing, Vol. 1, p. 81.

54
Grenadier and Voltigeur of the 94th Regiment

A. Grenadier. This painting represents a departure from the norm of the Manuscript because it depicts two different types of rank-and-file soldiers from the same line regiment at the same time (a circumstance only matched in Plates No. 29 and 59). This Grenadier is dressed as might be expected, but the arrangement of his cap cords is somewhat unusual, the lowest point in the drape of the cords seeming to be at the front of the bearskin and not on the left side, where it appears in all other examples. This appearance may, however, simply be the result of the artist's recurring problems with the techniques of perspective.

B. Voltigeur. On the strength of this and the previous figures of Voltigeurs it seems reasonable to conclude that a yellow collar trimmed with red, green epaulettes (with or without coloured crescents) and a sabre with green sword knot (with or without coloured trim) were the distinctions worn by most Voltigeurs, even though none of these were officially recognized by the military administration of the day. There is less consistency with respect to shako ornaments, but even so a green plume with yellow tip is relatively common, although the round yellow pom-pom is not. The use of entirely yellow cords is, however, uncommon. Also unusual is the form of shako plate which, like that of the 21st Regiment, is a precursor of the style formally adopted for all troops in 1812. The shield on which the regimental number appears is, however, much larger than similar devices on other surviving examples of this type of plate, and the position of the eagle itself is proportionately higher in relation to the base. Note that the chinscales have in this instance been tied up over the visor rather than over the plate as is the case in all the other illustrations of shakos so equipped.

Grenadier et Voltigeur du 94ᵐᵉ Reg:

55
Sapper of the 95th Regiment

This figure (and the others of the 95th Regiment which follow) provides another splendid opportunity for verifying the accuracy of the work of the Otto artist because there happens to exist a watercolour painting (hereinafter referred to as the 'Nuremberg Source') of figures of the 95th Line in Nuremberg in 1806 which precisely corroborates the two most peculiar features of the uniform of this Sapper and which is otherwise consistent on several less controversial points.[1] The two features referred to are, of course, the half-moon pocket on the front of the apron and the three tassels at the bottom of the same piece of equipment, and both appear in the Nuremberg painting as well. The Nuremberg-source Sapper does not have light blue lapels, in fact it seems likely that he is not wearing lapels at all, but has been depicted wearing the apron over a single-breasted coat, so this difference is not significant. On the other hand, the Nuremberg Source does clearly show musicians of the 95th with light blue collars and cuffs, a circumstance which makes it relatively easy to believe that the lapels of the full dress uniform of the Sapper might be light blue as well.

The list of other consistent points between the uniform depicted in this painting and the Sapper uniform depicted by the Nuremberg Source is impressive: red plume, white cords, red epaulettes, red crossed-axe sleeve badge, axe belt with square brass buckle and crossed-axe ornament, and musket slung over the back. Even the shape of the axes is similar (although not identical). The only obvious difference between the two figures is that the Nuremberg Sapper is wearing white gaiters. In this painting and many others in the Otto series the line of piping which begins under each lapel and which, presumably, would continue along the edge of the turnbacks is so thin that it is easy to miss.

1 This painting, which is apparently now in the Brunon Collection of the French Army Museum, has been the subject of two detailed articles by Rigo: 'Le 95e de Ligne – Nos ancêtres en Uniformes', *Tradition* No. 37 (February 1990), pp. 14–19, and No. 38 (March 1990), pp. 34–39 (the second part of this series being hereinafter referred to as Rigo, 'Le 95e de Ligne (2e partie)'). It was also the subject of an earlier article by J. Margerand in *Carnet de La Sabretache* for 1903, pp. 276–281, and at that time the painting was said to be in the Print Collection of the French National Library.

56
Officer and Grenadier of the 95th Regiment

A. Officer. There is no officer of Grenadiers depicted in the Nuremberg Source of the 95th, but there are several other officers in undress jackets. None of these is distinctly different from the uniform of this officer, but they all seem to have red piping down the front and white lining for the coat tails. One of the Nuremberg officers sports a sabre carried on a shoulder belt, and all are wearing boots featuring the same tapered brown 'cuff' as those in the Otto Manuscript. A nearly exact match exists, however, between the uniform of this figure and that of the Grenadier officer depicted in the 1807 edition of C.-F. Weiland's uniform prints.

B. Grenadier. The Nuremberg Source is consistent with this depiction of a Grenadier in that it also has a figure wearing a bearskin cap with white cords and a brass plate decorated with a grenade ornament, but it does not show either the visor or the chinscales which are prominent here. However, both sources agree that there was no cording across the front of the bearskin, another unusual coincidence. The cap cords of this figure have two raquettes on the right side, while only a single one seems to be shown in the Nuremberg Source. More importantly, although no Grenadier cuffs are fully visible in the Nuremberg Source, none of the other figures in that work has cuff flaps, an uncommon circumstance which is echoed in this painting in that the cuff opening is marked by three buttons and a parallel line of red piping, but no true flap.

57
Sapper of the 96th Regiment

The unique uniform of this Sapper defies detailed analysis because so little is reminiscent of other styles and forms of dress worn in the French Army. It may be that the facing colour is *rouge garance*, the colour specified for the collars and cuffs of the 96th in the White Uniform Regulations, but the cut of the coat, which seems to anticipate the style adopted by the French in 1812, suggests that the uniform itself was a foreign acquisition obtained from either Prussian or Duchy of Warsaw stores. The rising expanse of oversized fur busby, the flaring shape of the blade of the axe and the dark brown apron are also unusual features, none of which can be precisely traced. A print by Roger Forthoffer based on unspecified material in the *Collections of Herbert Knötel* shows a Sapper in similar uniform, but this time both jacket and the busby have a more traditional French look.[1] A final point about this painting is that it is one of the two in the Manuscript depicting a slung musket whose stock appears on the opposite side to the musket's barrel. Given the distances involved, this firearm must have been even shorter than a standard cavalry carbine.

1 R. Forthoffer, *Fiche Documentaire* No. 60 – *Infanterie de Ligne 1806–1809*.

58
Drum Major of the 96th Regiment

The uniform of this Drum Major is nearly identical with that of the Drum Major of the 75th Regiment, with the substitution of a nine button blue surtout for the red lapelled coat. Ironically, the more sombre the basic uniform, the more striking is the effect of the gold ornaments and trim, which in this instance have been enhanced by a pair of immense gold epaulettes in place of the more modest trefoil shoulder-straps worn by the other figure. Even the Drum Major's cross of the Legion of Honour shows up more prominently in this setting. The thick white waistbelt seems almost incongruously plain in this ensemble and it is accentuated by a hefty square buckle featuring silver details. The exact shape of the central device is unrecognizable, but one can see with difficulty that it bears the number '96' in gold. The mace carried by this figure appears to have a slightly different style of silver chain wrapped around its staff compared to those of the other Drum Majors in the Manuscript. The red plume on the bicorne hat is thicker and, apparently, more pliable than other plumes in the Manuscript.

59

[Grenadier and Fusilier of the] 96th Regiment

A. Grenadier. The rich but subtle diversity in Napoleonic uniforms is well-evidenced by the slight differences in detail which characterize the Line Grenadier figures in the Manuscript who are wearing bearskin caps. Of the six figures in this category, no two have exactly the same head-dress even though all of them look superficially similar. For instance, the cap of this figure has the same plate and plume as the Grenadier of the 95th Regiment, but it lacks the latter's visor and chinscales while it adds an additional white cord across the front. The uniform is otherwise unexceptional, although the vest does appear to have unusual pockets with silver buttons.

B. Fusilier. This figure probably comes closer than any other in the Manuscript to illustrating the uniform of the 'average' soldier in Napoleon's service during the period after adoption of the shako and prior to the introduction of the sweeping dress changes of 1812. The only touch of distinctiveness is to be found in the flat circular pom-pom consisting of a red border around a blue centre bearing the numeral '7'. At this period, the seven Fusilier companies of each battalion were numbered one to eight, with the number two not being used because that was the company replaced by the Voltigeur company in 1805.[1] The use of this style of pom-pom suggests that in the 96th Regiment the same colour scheme was used for all the pom-poms in the same battalion, differentiation between companies being achieved by use of the identifying numerals. This scheme would permit the different battalions of the same regiment to be identified from a distance, a situation which was not possible when the only distinctions were derived from the identifying colours of the pom-poms.

The junction of the cords on the left-hand side of the shako seems closer to the front of the shako than is typical, but this is probably a mistake by the Otto artist. More surprising is the presence of a second thin vertical line of cording dropping down from that junction to what appears to be a silver button located approximately where one would expect to see the boss for one side of the chinscales. As usual, there is no trace of the bayonet case which should be attached to the single shoulder belt. Also as usual, this Fusilier is clean shaven.

---

1 The numbering of companies prior to the introduction of Voltigeurs is confirmed by Colonel Trefcon's *Carnet*, pp. 22–23, and the substitution of the Voltigeurs for Fusilier company No. 2 is prescribed by Article I of the Imperial Decree of the 2nd Complementary Day of Year 13 (20 September 1805) in the *Journal Militaire* for Year 13, Part 2, p. 226. See, to the same effect, the schematic battalion diagram in Rigo, 'Le 95e de Ligne (2e partie)', at p. 39 (with accompanying text at p. 34, n. 3).

96ᵐᵉ Regiment

60
Officer and Voltigeur of the 96th Regiment

A. Officer. This Officer is the most sombre figure in the Manuscript because he lacks both the gorget and the turned-over boots worn by most other officers that could provide a minimum colour contrast for his uniform. The black waistbelt, which has an unusual round belt plate apparently decorated with an eagle device, contributes to the overall effect. The yellow collar seems to have piping along the sides of its central opening, but this piping is not clearly continued along the top edge. The short tapered green pompon on the bicorne hat has a peculiar yellow tip.

B. Voltigeur. The uniform of this Voltigeur demonstrates the extent to which dress in the field could deviate from official models. The bureaucrats in the Ministry of War never ceased to complain that Voltigeurs were entitled to no other dress distinctions than the prescribed chamois collar.[1] It is apparent that they could not have been aware of what the Colonel of the 96th Regiment had dreamt up. The shako seems unusually tall, a circumstance that increases the visual impact of the bands of yellow lace around the crown and base and formed into chevrons on the side. The green cords have yellow accents and there

is an extra vertical length of cord on the left side (similar to that on the Fusilier shako in the preceding Plate) running down to a silver button.[2] The small green pom-pom seems relatively modest given all the other ornamentation. The collar does not seem to have the traditional red piping, but there is a thin red line in the middle of the yellow crescents on the epaulettes. The most novel feature of the uniform, however, is the yellow cuff flap. (On the evidence of Martinet Plate No. 3, this bit of whimsy, although without red trim, was also used as a distinction by the 122nd Line.) This use of the distinctive Voltigeur colour elsewhere than on the collar is also confirmed for the 33rd Regiment by a statement in the Memoirs of General François Roguet that the newly formed Voltigeurs of that unit had 'yellow on their collars and cuffs'.[3]

---

1. See, e.g, a decree of 27 October 1807 forbidding voltigeurs to be armed with infantry sabres (*Journal Militaire* for 1807, Part 2, p. 113).
2. This feature is more easily viewed in the copy of this painting which appears as figure 25 on Rousselot Plate No. 17: *Infanterie de Ligne – Grenadiers et Voltigeurs 1804–813* (Paris 1943/1978).
3. *Mémoires Militaires du Lt.-Générale Comte Roguet, Colonel en second des Grenadiers à pied de la Vieille Garde* (4 vols., Paris 1862–65), Vol. 3, p. 165.

Officier et Voltigeur du 96ᵐᵉ Reg:

PART III
LIGHT INFANTRY AND NON-LINE TROOPS

PART III
LIGHT INFANTRY AND NON-LINE TROOPS

The infantry strength of the Grand Army included, in addition to the line infantry regiments, a number of other formations, the most numerous of which were the so-called Light infantry regiments, the descendants of the foot Chasseur regiments of the *Ancien Régime*. In theory these were regiments that were given special training so as to be better able to engage in skirmishing activity and to perform scouting and other duties of light troops. In practice, the only differences between Line and Light units were ones of dress and nomenclature and they were brigaded together and used interchangeably on the battlefield. By October 1806, there were 27 Light regiments numbered from 1 to 32, with five numbers vacant (11, 19, 20, 29 and 30).[1] Each had at least three battalions of nine companies each.[2] One company was of Carabiniers (the equivalent of line Grenadiers), one was of Voltigeurs and the remaining seven were styled as Chasseurs (the equivalent of line Fusiliers).

The basic uniform of the Light Infantry is described in detail in the *État Militaire* for Year X (1801–2):[3]

'Uniform. – Jacket [*habit-veste*] of dark blue cloth, with "Hungarian-style", triangular blue lapels piped with white; blue cuffs piped white; red collar, blue vest, blue trousers; half-gaiters, hat or shako with small tuft [*houpette*]; button with the number of the unit.'

The most distinctive aspect of this uniform was the predominance of the colour blue, but it also differed from that of the Line infantry in the shape of the lapels and in the fact that the tails of the jacket were cut significantly shorter (in theory, at least, to allow freer movement by the wearer). Light infantry soldiers also wore a different pattern of gaiter cut to mid-calf and usually decorated with coloured trim and a tassel around its upper edge. The Light infantry received the shako as its official head-dress in 1801, far in advance of the rest of the army, but these early models generally lacked shako plates and were shorter than those that appeared later in the period.[4] Since Light regiments had white metal buttons, the rank distinctions of their officers were silver rather than gold. (It is sometimes difficult to tell in the Manuscript when the artist is trying to depict the colour silver because his only technique for creating that colour is to add a blue-grey wash to white.)

The dress distinctions among the various companies in a Light regiment were similar to those in Line units, except that even the centre company Chasseurs (the equivalent of Line Fusiliers) had the epaulettes and sabres so characteristic of élite formations. The Carabiniers wore bearskin caps, red cords, plumes, epaulettes and other distinctions like their Grenadier brethren, but, despite their name, they were armed with standard infantry muskets and not with any special model of firearm. Voltigeurs in Light infantry units, like those in the Line, were theoretically limited to the distinctions of a sabre and a chamois collar, but in practice a similarly wide array of ornaments were tolerated. They were supposed to be armed with a light, Dragoon model musket, in order to facilitate their special tactic of riding into action mounted behind cavalrymen, but such muskets were as rarely seen as the tactic itself.[5] Chasseurs had the same red collar as the Carabiniers, but elsewhere made as much use as possible of combinations of green and red.

Another significant portion of the military strength of France was provided by the troops '*hors ligne*' (literally, 'outside the line'), soldiers in the pay of the Emperor who were not typically expected to serve in the line of battle. Some of these units, such as the Corsican Tirailleurs and the Tirailleurs of the Po, had superior records in action, but others, like the Municipal Guard of the City of Paris, spent most of their time in non-combatant roles. The Paris Guard, which was formed in 1802[6] with a strength of two regiments of infantry (each sub-divided into two battalions) and one squadron of dragoons, had the express role of providing security services for the city of Paris. With the prospect of a winter campaign in Poland in the offing, however, Napoleon did not hesitate to draw on this reserve of trained manpower by calling in December 1806 for a provisional unit formed from elements of each of the two infantry regiments to join the Grand Army for active service.

The decree creating the Paris Guard is very specific on the subject of its uniforms:

'XXV. The form of the head-dress, coat and shoes of the two regiments of infantry of the Municipal Guard of Paris will be the same as that established for line infantry.

The first regiment will have a green coat lined with white, white vest and trousers, black gaiters and red collar, cuffs and lapels.

The second regiment will have a red coat, white vest and trousers, green cuffs, collar and lapels and black gaiters.'

The red uniform of the Second Regiment was sufficiently unique that they were dubbed the 'crayfish' by the rest of the Grand Army.[7]

One special peculiarity of the initial organization of the Paris Guard was that there were only five companies in each battalion, and none of these was supposed to have élite status. None the less, given the manifest desire of the average Napoleonic soldier for the outward trappings of special status, it should not be surprising to find that the researches of Rigo in the French Army archives have established that Grenadier companies were created in the Paris Guard as early as 1803.[8] By an Imperial Decree of 18 May 1806, the strength of each regiment was increased by an additional élite company, which seems to have received a Chasseur designation despite the fact that the regiments were otherwise styled as line formations.[9]

1   Belhomme, Vol. 4, p. 345. The vacant numbers are from P.-C. Alombert and J. Colin, *La Campagne de 1805 en Allemagne* (6 vols., Paris 1902–1908), Vol. 1, pp. 7–8 (hereafter referred to as 'Alombert & Colin').

2   The wording of the order creating companies of Voltigeurs in light infantry regiments, which was handed down over one year prior to their creation in line regiments, seems to imply that the new company would be an addition to the strength of each unit and not a replacement for an existing company, thus making a total of ten companies. See Order of 22 Ventose Year XII (13 March 1804) (the 'Voltigeur Order'), *Correspondance de Napoléon 1er*, Vol. 9, pp. 287–289, and Belhomme, Vol. 4, p. 287. Nevertheless, the number of companies seems to have reverted to nine prior to the campaign of 1805. See 'Composition of Light Infantry' in Alombert & Colin, Vol. 1, pp. 122–123.

3   Quoted in Marchal, *Les Uniformes*, p. 10.

4   See the description of the light infantry shako in the Equipment List, *Journal Militaire* for Year X, Pt. 1, p. 174.

5   Voltigeur Order, Articles 7 and 8.

6   Order of 12 Vendemiaire Year 11 (4 October 1802), *Journal Militaire* for Year 11, Pt. 1, pp. 19–29.

7   L.C. Coqueugniot, *Histoire de la Légion du Nord – Mémoire de L.C. Coqueugniot, Major* (Beauchevain, Belgium 1992), p. 98. This work is a reprint by Bernard Coppens of a memoir which origi-

nally appeared in the *Nouvelle Revue Rétrospective* in 1898.

8 *Le Plumet* Plate U14: *Garde Municipale de Paris – 1er et 2e Régiments–1807, Dragons–1808.*

9 The terminology used in connection with these new companies is a source of significant confusion in the relevant secondary sources, but once again the research of Rigo appears to provide a definitive answer in that he found records confirming the existence of a Chasseur company in the first regiment in 1807. However, Bernard Coppens, a Belgian Napoleonic expert, has found that the *Annuaire de Dèpartement de la Seine pour 1808* refers to a Voltigeur company in the first regiment and a Chasseur company in the second. See text to Coppens Plate G.T.2: *Garde de Paris – 2e Régiment d'Infanterie 1807.*

61

Grenadier [Carabinier] Officer of the
9th Regiment of Foot Chasseurs [Light Infantry]

Since there were no French regiments of Foot Chasseurs other than the Imperial Guard, this painting undoubtedly depicts an officer of the 9th Regiment of Light Infantry, and since there were no Grenadiers in the light infantry, the officer equally undoubtedly belongs to the Carabinier company of that unit.[1] Despite the normal limitations of perspective, the Otto artist has in this case managed to render both the front and the back of the bearskin at the same time, thereby providing a rare contemporary glimpse of the adornment of the calotte (literally, the skull cap), a round patch of cloth found at the top of the back of each cap normally quartered by a white cross into alternating red and blue segments.[2] In this depiction, however, both visible segments are red, the cross appears to be blue (and has been so described by both Rigo and Rousselot) and there is a ring of white or silver lace around the outside edge.

The rest of the uniform is relatively standard, although, as always, there are certainly some points of interest such as the collar with blue instead of white piping. The most unusual feature, however, is the cuff flap with four buttons, but that arrangement is also to be found on the coat of an officer of the 12th Light in the French Army Museum and in depictions of soldiers of the 3rd Light Regiment in a manuscript from Lüneburg, Germany which can also be dated to 1807.[3] The gorget and belt buckle of a Light Infantry officer would more typically have been made of silver, but the raised grenade on each is appropriate for a Carabinier. The sabre belt apparently has a second strap in front to hold the scabbard in place, but this configuration is inconsistent with surviving examples of such belts. The sabre itself is another Otto gem with its intricate damascening. A final light infantry touch is the hussar-style boots with silver trim.

1   Both Rigo and Rousselot have made the same attribution. See *Le Plumet* Plate U7: *Infanterie Légère, 9e Régiment, Voltigeurs, Carabiniers et Chasseurs 1804–1808*, and '9e Régiment d'Infanterie Légère–1807' in *Carnet de la Sabretache* No. 22 (2nd Trimester 1974), p. 55 and plate.

2   The regulation description of the *calotte* (also sometimes called the '*cul de singe*', or monkey's bottom) is given in the List of Equipment Dimensions at p. 175.

3   A photograph of the officer's coat appears in Willing, Vol. 1, p. 85. The location of the original paintings constituting the Lüneburg Manuscript is unknown today, but copies of these paintings exist and were reproduced in *Zeitschrift fur Heereskunde* (1953), pp. 67–72 and 87–89. The paintings are also copied in Rousselot Plate No. 33: *Infanterie Légère 1804–1813* (Paris 1966).

62

Grenadier [Carabinier] and Fusilier [Chasseur] of the 9th Regiment of Foot Chasseurs [Light Infantry]

A. Carabinier. The uniform of this Carabinier soldier differs in many respects from that of his officer in the preceding Plate. While the bearskin cap and plume are the same, the double cords looping from (high to low) left to right, instead of vice versa, are quite unusual. The jacket has no visible coat tails, a circumstance which indicates that this feature barely covered the seat of the soldier. The red cuff flaps here have only three buttons and, moreover, a scalloped edge piped blue. The white trim around the entire length of the shoulderpiece of the red epaulette cannot be found elsewhere in the Manuscript, but can also be seen in Martinet Plate No. 265 illustrating a Carabinier in post–1812 uniform. The white waistcoat is a prominent feature of any light infantry uniform, and this one is characterized by buttons on the flap of the waistcoat pocket. The trim on the top edge of the short gaiters is, unexpectedly, white with a red tassel instead of red throughout. The firearm seems to be a standard line infantry Charleville rather than a special light infantry model.

B. Chasseur. There is a real human contrast in this painting between the tall, moustachioed Carabinier and this younger-looking, shorter and clean-shaven Chasseur. Almost by way of making up for his shorter stature, he sports an extremely tall shako, by the standards of early models of that head-dress, topped by an even taller plume rising out of a tufted pom-pom. The arrangement of shako cords looks to be distinctly asymmetrical, but this may merely be the result of the artist's optimistic attempt to show the cords on both the left and right sides simultaneously. There is also on the left side the same thin cord running straight down to a button which was found on the shakos of the Voltigeur and Fusilier of the 96th Line Regiment, but in this instance it is complemented by a hanging tassel.[1] Given the use of white metal buttons by the light infantry, one might expect this shako plate to have been silver as well, but there are other known instances of this type of anomaly.[2] In any event, the plate does not bear even the suggestion of the regimental number. The combination of red and green for the distinguishing epaulettes, sword knot and tassels of a Chasseur is relatively common, but the blue trim on his collar (and that of the Carabinier) is not.

---

1 A photograph of the left side of a shako of the Guard Sailors which appears in Willing, Vol. 1, p. 65, shows the only example of this feature known to the author outside the Otto Manuscript.

2 The 8th, 17th and 26th Light Infantry also had yellow metal plates according to Blondieau, *Aigles et Shakos*, p. 18.

Grenadier & Fusilier du 9.me Reg. des Chasseur à pié.

63

Sapper of the 10th Regiment of Foot Chasseurs [Light Infantry]

The caption to this painting, like that of Plates No. 61 and 65, is written by two different hands and employs a more modern spelling of the word 'pied' than that which appears in the unaltered caption to Plate No. 62. These circumstances constitute almost irrefutable proof that some of the paintings have been cut down from their original size. What we do not know for certain is whether the cropping removed from the painting another figure or merely some superfluous landscape.

This Sapper has adopted the same type of fur busby worn by members of the élite companies of Hussars and Chasseurs, with its distinctive red cloth 'bag'. The coat is simply that of a Carabinier, although with the traditional crossed axe badge on the sleeve and the epaulettes embellished with white trim on each side of the crescents. As can be glimpsed near the tip of the sabre, the costume is completed with blue trousers and short gaiters with red trim (and, presumably, a red tassel) around the top. The belting and other equipment is similar to that for Line Sappers and, indeed, the axe is an almost perfect (although slighter smaller) copy of that carried by the Sapper of the 94th Regiment in Plate No. 53. The sidearm, however, is unique because it represents the only appearance in the Otto Manuscript of the regulation Sapper sabre-saw.[1] The musket, which here is supported by a rather slack sling, does not resemble any French model of short firearm because the barrel does not extend noticeably past the top muzzle band, so perhaps this was a foreign acquisition.[2]

---

1 A photograph of a surviving example of this type of weapon can be found in Willing, Vol. 1, p. 81.
2 For instance, based on the limited amount of evidence available, this weapon might be an Austrian cavalry carbine of the type illustrated in Willing, Vol. 2, p. 62.

64

Sapper of the 16th Regiment [of] Chasseurs [Light Infantry]

The figure in this painting is, by a wide margin, the most outlandish and most mysterious in the Otto Manuscript. Nevertheless, as with any Otto painting there are enough verifiable details to ensure that those details that are not verifiable must still be taken seriously. Starting with the shako, the tall red plume and upper and lower red bands are familiar enough, although the use of white rather than red cords to complete the ensemble seems odd. The beautifully detailed shako plate displaying the regimental number inside a hunting horn is appropriately silver and is almost identical in form with a surviving plate of the 14th Light Regiment.[1] The semi-circular black shape in the front of the shako is puzzling unless one assumes that it represents a detachable visor of the sort worn on some early models of shako. If that is the case, there is no indication of how it was attached to the shako, although on some models three hooks were normally used for the purpose. Remarkably, one of the Zimmerman drawings, while differing in many other details, shows a soldier of the 16th Light wearing precisely this type of visor (although again there is no visible means of attachment).

The rest of the uniform is more problematical, because only the epaulettes and the sabre are recognizably French items. The use of light purple as a facing colour is less unprecedented than the shape of the lapels, but the combination of the two is unique, as is the use of blue grenades to ornament the collar.[2] Even the arm patch has its own novel design of axes crossed over the symbol of a grenade. The facing colour appears again on the breeches in a scalloped edge line of lace down the outside seam, but the trim of the short gaiters is, mercifully, plain red. Certainly the most striking visual effect of the uniform derives from the black leather gauntlet gloves and apron, the former being an item seen elsewhere in Napoleonic iconography only as a high fashion affectation of light cavalry officers. No other Napoleonic soldier, however, was ever seen wearing anything like this green cartridge box on a green waist-belt accented with light green stitching. The straight shape of the axe blade is uncommon but similar to that carried by the Sapper of the 3rd regiment in Plate No. 22. The narrow width of the belt for the axe case, however, is unprecedented.

1 Willing, Vol. 1, p. 86.
2 Both Rousselot ('16e Léger 1807–1808' in *Carnet de la Sabretache* N. S. No. 24 (4th Trimester 1974), pp. 107–108) and Rigo (*Le Plumet* Plate No. 191: *Infanterie Légère et Étrangère – Sapeurs des 10e et 16e Régiments, Bataillon Neufchâtel, 3e Suisse 1808–1812*) assert without supporting evidence that this jacket was inspired by Württemberg military fashions.

Sappeur du 16.ᵐᵉ Reg: Chasseurs

65
Drum Major of the 16th Regiment of Foot Chasseurs [Light Infantry]

Like the Drum Major of the 96th Regiment in Plate No. 58, this figure seems to be wearing an undress uniform that is more subdued than would be the case for full dress, but which nevertheless is made striking by the addition of judicious amounts of metallic braid. The plume of the bicorne hat has a white over red colour combination which is extremely rare, and ribbon chin straps tied up at the back in the same way as depicted in Plates No. 33 (Officer and Voltigeur of the 21st Regiment) and No. 34 (Officer and Fusilier of the 21st Regiment). The silver lace around the collar and cuffs is ornamented with a delicate filigree, but the repetition of this detail on the rank stripes is unexpected. It also seems odd that the same filigree does not accompany the silver lace on the inside of the cuff on the right sleeve of the figure. The chamois (buff) trousers are obviously a campaign wear item, but the hussar boots with thick silver trim and tassel would probably have been worn in full dress as well. Some of the other Drum Majors illustrated in the Manuscript have sabres with silver fittings which would be more appropriate for this figure than the one he carries, but in any event it is unexpected to find a plain red sword knot rather than one of silver or gold.

66

Grenadier [Carabinier] and Chasseur [Voltigeur] of the 16th Regiment [of Light Infantry]

A. Carabinier. The distinctive colour red combined with a light infantry style uniform creates the certainty that the figure on the left of this painting is indeed a Carabinier, and not a Grenadier as indicated by the caption. In contrast to the Carabinier of the 9th Light in Plate No. 62, instead of a bearskin he is wearing the same type of shako as the regimental Sapper, so he has the same peculiar visor, but the shako has red cords instead of white and a silver grenade ornament has been substituted for the Sapper's shako plate. The strip of lace which holds the cockade in place was probably white originally, but has become discoloured over time.[1] The shako cords of both figures in this painting have the same vertical line of cording running to a button at the base of the shako first discussed above in connection with the head-dress of the Fusilier and Voltigeur of the 96th Line Regiment. Both figures also have four-button cuff flaps, but a significant array of other contemporary sources suggests that this was by no means an uncommon variation for light infantry uniforms.[2] The rest of the uniform is as might be expected.

B. Voltigeur. Despite the caption to this painting, the prominence of chamois (or buff) in the colour scheme of the uniform suggests that the figure depicted is a Voltigeur and not a Chasseur. In this regard, the buff cuff flap and the buff gaiter trim with green tassel are particularly noteworthy, as is, for other reasons, the white instead of buff cording. The green and red epaulettes and the sabre knot do, however, look like standard Chasseur issue.

1 Rousselot has asserted that the round metal bit below the red cords in the centre of the shako is in fact a button attached to such lace, rather than a portion of the grenade ornament, but that assertion is intriguing rather than convincing. L. Rousselot, '16e Légère 1807–1808', *Carnet de la Sabretache* N.S. No. 24 (4th Trimester 1974), pp. 107–108, at 108.
2 In addition to the examples cited in Note 2 in the text accompanying Plate No. 61 above, four button flaps are also found in Weiland's plate of a Light Infantry Chasseur reproduced in Michel Pétard's article 'L'Homme de 1804 – Le Chasseur d'Infanterie Légère', *Uniformes* No. 49 (Jan./Feb. 1979), pp. 20–26, at 22, and in an amateur Bavarian painting of a Carabinier in 1806 reproduced in Jean-Claude Quennevat's *Les Vrais Soldats de Napoléon* (Brussels 1966), p. 93.

Grenadier et Chasseur
du 16.me Reg:

67
Drum Major and Chasseur of the Guard of Paris

A. Drum Major. The research work of Rigo has established that, of the two Drum Majors of the Paris Guard, only that of the Second Regiment was included in the composite force which joined the Grand Army in 1807.[1] So this painting is in all likelihood a portrait of one Jean Dominique Bertholde, an Italian who enlisted as Drum Major of the Second Regiment of the Municipal Guard in May of 1803. Given the lavishness of many Drum Major uniforms, this one is almost remarkably restrained, since it consists of the basic coat of the regiment adorned with gold epaulettes and one modest band of gold trim around the collar and cuffs. The facings of the coat should be green, but the shade is so dark (whether by intent or by darkening of the colour over time) that these features actually look more black or blue. The lapels seem to have red piping, but the absence of that piping across the top of the lapel may be an indication that the artist actually intended this feature to be gold as well (which would be more in keeping with the scheme of modest distinctions), although he failed to carry out this intention in practice. Two other small points about this figure are of interest: (1) the absence of any cuff flap and (2) the buttons on the pockets of the waistcoat.

B. Chasseur. As noted above, the Paris Guard was unique in having one of its élite companies styled as Chasseurs, and the Otto Manuscript is one of the few contemporary sources that correctly reports this oddity. For the First Regiment, however, the unhappy sartorial result of this designation was the wearing of green distinctions with a green uniform. The bearskin appears to be the same as that of the Chasseurs of the Imperial Guard, though with green cords instead of white, and it therefore has double raquettes and a cockade at the base of the plume. The most controversial feature of the jacket is the green piping around all the red facings, because such piping is not mentioned in the regulations and is absent from a surviving jacket of the First Regiment in the French Army Museum, but does show up in the paintings of the First Regiment in the Hamburg Manuscript.[2] The jacket is also missing the traditional three buttons under the right lapel which can be seen clearly on the jackets in the next Plate. The red, rather than green, sabre knot is unexpected, as are the brass bands on the musket.

1   *Le Plumet* Plate No. 242: *Infanterie – Tambour-Majors des 16e et 75e de Ligne et du 2e Régiment de la Garde de Paris.* According to his service record, Bertholde would, at 6 feet 3 inches tall, have been a veritable giant for his day, but that unusual height is not apparent by comparison to the height of the Chasseur.
2   Note, however, that Weiland's plate of a Grenadier of the First Regiment shows white piping.

174

Tambour major
de la Garde de
Paris

Chasseur   de la Gar[de]
                        de Paris

68
Officer and Grenadier of the Guard of Paris

A. Officer. The red coat proves conclusively that this officer belongs to the Second Regiment of the Paris Guard, and his bearskin proves equally that he is a member of that unit's élite company of Grenadiers. The facings appear to be black, but given the unanimity of sources that declare that the distinctive colour of the Second Regiment was dark green, this appearance must be the result of decomposition of the pigments since the painting was created. (This conclusion is further supported by the fact that these facings do not appear to be any darker than the colour of the jacket worn by the Chasseur in the preceding Plate.) They are outlined in red piping as confirmed by Plate No. 86 of the Hamburg Manuscript, although Weiland shows white piping.[1] The gilt cords and cap plate seem to be distinctly lighter in colour than the similar features in other paintings, but this circumstance may simply be the result of a difference in pigments used from one picture to the next rather than the intentional depiction of a feature of the Paris Guard uniforms. This figure also has waistcoat pockets closed by buttons, and the waistcoat itself is cut sufficiently to allow it to fall over the black waistbelt. The elegant belt buckle is similar to that worn by the Grenadier Officer of the Guard.

B. Grenadier. The bearskin cap of this figure has standard white cords but it also has the atypical feature of the cockade appearing below the plume. The red epaulettes provide little distinction against the red background of the uniform, which is why many of the other red-coated units in the French Army (such as the Swiss and Hanoverians) opted for epaulettes of other colours such as white and blue. There has been an obvious deterioration of pigment on the left of the figure, because both the sleeve and the epaulette on that side appear to be the same colour (darker than on the right) and the white knapsack strap has become the same shade of red as well. The cross-belts are somewhat off-centre, which gives a good view of the right-hand skirt of the jacket, and it is surprising that the beginning of the white turnback is not visible farther up. In this painting the artist has been guilty of two notable lapses – a small portion of the knapsack visible under the right arm has not been coloured in and the shape of the hand resting on the right hip of the Grenadier looks distinctly unnatural. Like the Chasseur of the First Regiment in the preceding Plate, this figure carries a musket with brass bands.

---

1 Facsimiles of the two Weiland Plates relating to the Guard of Paris are reproduced in Emmanuel Martin, 'La Garde de Paris (1802–1813)', *Carnet de la Sabretache* (1903), pp. 1–7. These two sources, along with the illustrations of the uniforms of this Regiment to be found in Martinet and the Bourgeois of Hamburg are discussed in Lucien Rousselot, 'Garde de Paris', *Carnet de la Sabretache* No. 12 (New Series, 1972), p. 39.

Officier et Grenadier
de la Garde de
Paris

PART IV
LINE CAVALRY

PART IV
LINE CAVALRY

The mounted forces of the Grand Army of 1807 were effectively divided into three primary classifications reflecting Napoleon's conception of the three different roles to be played by cavalry in his campaigns, a conception he put into practice by concentrating his cavalry whenever possible into autonomous formations operating independently from the infantry.[1] The most familiar of these is the light cavalry, the Hussars and Chasseurs, led into history by such renowned commanders as Lasalle, Pajol, Montbrun and the Colbert brothers, whose job was to screen the advance of the French army and seek out the enemy before battle and then pursue them relentlessly after the battle had been won. Next is the heavy cavalry, the Cuirassiers and Carabiniers under Nansouty and Hautpoul, which represented the most potent form of shock weapon available to deliver a battlefield *coup de grâce*. Last is the medium cavalry, consisting exclusively of the Dragoons of the line, a corps intended to combine the mobility of cavalry with the staying power of infantry and so able both to consolidate the gains made by light cavalry and to exploit those made by the heavy cavalry. (Sometimes, however, the hybrid role of the Dragoons seems to have combined the worst, rather than the best, of two worlds.)

The regimental distribution of the French line cavalry at this time was:[2]

> 2 regiments of Carabiniers
> 12 regiments of Cuirassiers
> 30 regiments of Dragoons
> 25 regiments of Mounted Chasseurs[3]
> 10 regiments of Hussars.

Cavalry regiments were decidedly smaller than infantry regiments in terms of numbers because of the expense involved in having to buy, equip and maintain horses in addition to paying, clothing and feeding the men. They were all sub-divided into four squadrons of two companies each, but the Dragoons and light cavalry had more officers and men (120 per company as opposed to 95 per company) per unit than the heavy cavalry to allow for the greater wastage they might suffer in performing their ordinary duties.[4] Generally one company in each regiment was designated as the élite company and was provided with some distinguishing uniform features such as bearskin caps or busbies, but this was not the case for the Carabiniers and the Cuirassiers because those regiments as a whole were considered to be élite formations.[5]

At one point it had been intended that every member of the élite company of each cavalry regiment would be equipped with a tool in addition to his weapons, one-third of the men to be issued with shovels, one-third picks and one-third axes.[6] This plan never reached fruition, but it undoubtedly is one of the reasons why many cavalry units equipped a small number of élite company troopers as Sappers to introduce additional glamour to the head of the regimental column. An unpublished history of the 17th Dragoons relates that in 1805 Colonel de Saint-Dizier of that unit was using all ten regimental Sappers as a special bodyguard.[7]

In contrast to the relatively standardized dress of the infantry, each type of cavalry had a different style of dress, every regiment within that type having its own uniquely identifiable uniform. The following are brief descriptions of each style:

1. Carabiniers. Befitting their status as members of the senior mounted regiments in the army, the Carabiniers all wore bearskin caps. Since they steadfastly refused to wear chin straps, however, the cap cords in these regiments actually served the functional purpose of preventing loss if and when the bearskin fell off, which is why one end of the cord was attached to a button on the jacket.[8] The other signature feature of the Carabinier uniform at this time was the buff belting with white trim. Both regiments wore blue jackets with red facings, but they could be distinguished from one another by the cuff flap, which was red piped blue for the first regiment and blue piped red for the second.[9]

2. Cuirassiers. It is ironic that the most radical change which Napoleon made in the dress of his cavalry was the creation in 1802-4 of the regiments of Cuirassiers wearing body armour and helmets more reminiscent of the Middle Ages than the 19th century. All the regiments wore a blue uniform jacket, the first six regiments having red facings and the second six having yellow facings.[10] The facings themselves were arranged in distinct patterns so that, in theory at least, each regiment could be distinguished from the others on this basis. Thus the First Regiment of Cuirassiers had red collars, cuffs, cuff flaps, lapels, turnbacks and pockets *en travers* (i.e., with the opening horizontal to the ground), the Second Regiment had the same except for a blue collar and blue

cuff flaps. The colour scheme of the Fourth Regiment was identical with that of the First, but this time the pockets were *en long* (i.e., having the opening perpendicular to the ground).

3. Dragoons. The most characteristic elements of the Dragoon uniform worn during the First Empire were the brass helmet and green coat which had remained constant since the days of the *Ancien Régime*.[11] The distinctions among regiments were created by the use of five facing colours: scarlet, crimson, pink, yellow and *aurore* — distributed in that order to groups of six regiments each and then worn in different combinations by each unit in the group with, once again, the location of the pocket in the coat tails being one of the variable features.[12]

4. Hussars. The Hussars were certainly the most showy regiments of the French Army, combining an exotic style of dress[13] with vivid colour combinations accentuated by a profusion of buttons and, literally, yards and yards of yellow or white braid. Each regiment was dressed according to a unique colour scheme which could even be varied from day to day depending on whether the unit was wearing the dolman or the pelisse, or both, or instead some undress jacket.[14]

5. Chasseurs. When the first Chasseur units were formed before the Revolution, their uniforms featuring braided jackets and breeches were distinctly reminiscent of those of the Hussars, although with the use of green as the basic uniform colour for all regiments. Gradually, however, Chasseur uniforms evolved in unique ways so that while some units retained a Hussar-style uniform, others came to emphasize a jacket with pointed lapels similar to that worn by the Guard Chasseurs, or one with no lapels at all which had a markedly modern look.[15] Because each facing colour for Chasseur uniforms was worn by only three regiments, they used more colours than the

Dragoons: scarlet, yellow, pink, crimson, orange, sky-blue, *aurore*, *capucine*, *garance* [Madder Red] and *amaranthe*.

The Otto Manuscript is perhaps most singularly weak in its depiction of French cavalry mounts and their harnesses, which further proves that the artist was not a cavalryman. The horses all have markedly small heads and are unnaturally posed. The saddlecloths are almost always misshapen, and the artist often omits the straps that would have held them in place. Some care is taken in each case to represent accurately the configuration of the bridle and reins, but usually the results do not withstand careful scrutiny. One minor but interesting related point is that all the stirrups on mounted figures in the Manuscript are shown hanging from narrow black straps. All modern sources and surviving artefacts show Napoleonic stirrup straps as having been white, but the Martinet plates are consistent with the Manuscript in this regard.

The unfamiliarity of the Otto artist with the mounted troops of the Grand Army is also obvious from the peculiar captions he provided for some of the paintings. For instance, Plate No. 69 bears the caption 'Cuirassier Grenadier' although the figure illustrated is certainly a Carabinier. The only plausible explanations for the mistake are that (1) the artist was unaware of the existence of the regiments of Carabiniers, (2) he consequently believed that any cavalryman in a blue coat must belong to a Cuirassier regiment and (3) he equally believed that any figure wearing a fur cap must be a member of the élite company of the relevant regiment. (Subsequent captions on the paintings of Hussars and Chasseurs confirm that the Otto artist believed that the term 'Grenadier' was appropriate for any élite company trooper.) This conclusion is further borne out by the fact that he has assigned the same saddle furnishings and regimental

number '21' to both this Carabinier and the figure in Plate No. 70, which is correctly identified as a Cuirassier.

This number is, of course, incorrect for either a Carabinier or a Cuirassier regiment. Rigo has attempted to explain this peculiarity by asserting that the figure in Plate No. 70 is one of the members of the 1st Cuirassiers who came over from the 21st Cavalry Regiment when the latter unit was disbanded in 1803.[16] His solution is questionable, however, because it (1) depends on the proposition that those transferees would still have been using their old regimental equipment four years after the transfer, and (2) ignores the fact that the Carabinier in Plate No. 69 has been given the same regimental number. Moreover, the uniform illustrated in Plate No. 70 is more consistent (because of the vertical pocket) with that of the 4th or 6th Cuirassiers than with that of the 1st Regiment.[17] Instead, one might equally well posit that the '21' is simply a deformation of the number '4' which resulted from the artist misreading the number in a preliminary sketch of the Cuirassier when he returned later to complete the painting. He then may simply have compounded the problem by being consistent in using this same wrong number for the Carabinier in consequence of his mistaken belief that both figures belonged to the same regiment. Unfortunately, this explanation, too, has at least one flaw, because the 4th Cuirassiers were not in the same division of heavy cavalry as the Carabiniers and it is therefore unlikely that the Otto artist would have seen them both at the same time. The mystery of the number '21' is therefore probably insoluble.

1   David Chandler, *The Campaigns of Napoleon* (New York 1966), pp. 352–355.

2   Leon de Jaquier, *La Cavalerie Française de 1800 à 1815* (Paris n.d.), pp. 13–15 (hereinafter 'Jaquier').

3   These regiments were numbered 1 to 27, with numbers 17 and 18 being vacant because the regiments were dissolved in 1794.

4   Jaquier, p. 24.
5   J. Margerand, 'Les Compagnies d'Élite de la Cavalerie', *Carnet de la Sabretache* (1926), pp. 358–364, at 361–362.
6   *Ibid.*, p. 362.
7   In the combat of Albeck on 11 October 1805, the 17th Dragoons charged a superior force of Austrian cavalry and the Colonel and three of his Sappers were killed. The other seven were wounded and captured, but freed by the Austrian general as a reward for their heroism. M. E. Gridel and Captain Richard, eds., *Cahiers de Vieux Soldats de la Révolution et de L'Empire* (Paris 1903), pp. 130–132.
8   See the illustrations of the back of the head-dress in Rousselot Plate No. 44: *Carabiniers 1804–1810*.
9   Michel Pétard, 'L'Homme de 1807 – Le Carabinier, grenadier des troupes à cheval', *Uniformes* No. 35 (January/February 1977), pp. 21–30, at p.23.
10 The best introduction to the cuirassier uniform is through Rousselot Plates No. 15: *Cuirassiers 1804–1810*, 37: *Cuirassiers 1810–1814*, 46: *Cuirassiers. Officiers. 1804–1815*, No. 91: *Cuirassiers – Trompettes 1804–1812*, and No. 102: *Cuirassiers –Trompettes 1804–1812 (II)*. Also required reading, however, is the remarkable special issue of *Tradition* magazine (Nos. 54–55, July/August 1991) devoted entirely to the Cuirassiers of the First Empire and featuring articles by Rigo and Michel Pétard and colour photographs of numerous artefacts and contemporary illustrations of Cuirassier uniforms.
11 One British officer was particularly impressed with the Dragoon headwear: 'The brazen helmet, with the lofty cone, black horse hair, and tiger-skin band, looked very noble...' Moyle Sherer, *Recollections of the Peninsula* (London 1823), p. 166. Another found that Dragoon helmets also still served a very useful, if primitive, purpose: 'I must mention that I received my wound in the act of uplifting my arm and making a cut at the head of my antagonist, on his near side. He wore a brass helmet, and the blade of my sabre broke in two on it, which left me quite at his mercy.' Bryan Perrett, ed., *A Hawk at War: The Peninsular Reminiscences of General Sir Thomas Brotherton, CB* (Chippenham, England 1986), p. 54.
12 Michel Pétard, 'L'Homme de 1807 – Le Dragon de la Ligne', *Uniformes* No. 87 (March/April 1985), pp. 21–24.
13 For a discussion of the origins of the traditional elements of Hussar dress, see D. de Noirmont, 'Historique de la Sabretache et des Autres Parties Characteristiques de Costume des Hussards', *Carnet de la Sabretache* (1895), pp. 252–262.
14 The colours of all the regiments are set forth in schematic form on Rousselot Plate No. 57: *Hussards 1804–1812* (Paris 1965).
15 Général Vanson, 'Études d'Uniformes: Les Chasseurs à Cheval', *Carnet de la Sabretache* Vol. 3 (1895), in three parts starting on pp. 32, 79 and 337.
16 Rigo, 'Les Cuirassiers 1804–1815: Les "Gros Frères" de L'Empereur', *Tradition* No. 54–55 (July/August 1991), pp. 12–26 at 20 (hereinafter referred to as Rigo, 'Les Cuirassiers').
17 Marchal, *Les Uniformes*, pp. 14–15.

69
Cuirassier Grenadier [Mounted Carabinier]

As is certain from the bearskin and the buff belts trimmed with white, this painting depicts a trooper from one of the Carabinier regiments. (Exact identification of the regiment is, of course, impossible because the distinguishing cuff flaps are hidden by the gauntlet gloves.) Carabiniers have been most often illustrated in their full dress jacket with red lapels and turnbacks (with blue grenade ornaments) and blue collar piped red, but the wearing of a single-button surtout on campaign has been well documented.[1] Surprisingly, however, there is no pocket in evidence in the coat tails. The white piping around the exterior of the epaulette shoulderpiece should continue across the epaulette strap, but this feature has been forgotten by the artist (together with the colouring of part of the shoulder belt contiguous to the epaulette.[2] With regard to the equipment of the Carabiniers, sources are unanimous in depicting the sabre as being carried from a single belt frog encompassing the throat of the scabbard, and not from two thin sabre straps as shown in this picture.[3] The artist has, however, correctly depicted the bayonet hanging from the waist-belt and the carrying position of the Dragoon-model musket.

There are a number of puzzling aspects in the horse furniture. First and foremost, as discussed at length above, the numeral '21' on the end of the portmanteau is clearly incorrect for a Carabinier. Although many sources show the portmanteau as having a cylindrical rather than rectangular shape, the latter was in fact regulation until approximately 1807–8, and should have been decorated with a grenade device.[4] The cloak on top of the portmanteau has been correctly arranged with its red lining prominently displayed, but there appears to be only a single strap (instead of three) holding it in place and that strap is white instead of black like the rest of the leatherwork. The saddle-cloth should certainly extend under the portmanteau to give protection to the horse's back.

1 There exists, for instance, a variant of Weiland's plate of a Carabinier which shows a dismounted trooper in a single-breasted jacket.
2 The thorn-like projection from the side of the plume may also be an error of the artist and not an intentional feature.
3 See, for example, the painting of the sword belt in Michel Pétard, 'L'Homme de 1807: Le Carabinier – Grenadier des Troupes à Cheval', *Uniformes* No. 35 (January/February 1977), pp. 21–30, at 27.
4 Rousselot Plate No. 44: *Carabiniers 1804–1810* (Paris 1967) and MacCarthy, *La Cavalerie Française*, p. 253.

Grenadier des Cuirassiers

70
Cuirassier

This is the only Plate that shows a regimental number in the painting but not in the caption, a circumstance which suggests that the Otto artist himself had some reservations about the accuracy of his identification of the non-existent 21st Cuirassiers. As noted above, the arrangement of the facings and pockets on the jacket of this figure make it more likely that he is intended to depict a trooper of the 4th or 6th Cuirassiers. No matter what regiment is represented in this painting, there are a number of interesting aspects of this figure's uniform and equipment. The helmet differs from all other surviving examples from the early Empire in that the forward edge of the yellow metal crest (which is completely visible here despite all the laws of artistic perspective) is unornamented instead of having some decoration which, in many cases, would include the regimental number.[1] No other contemporary source shows white piping on the coloured collar of a Cuirassier, but this decorative touch fits in well with the white edging to the red cuirass lining and might represent a scheme for distinguishing the two regiments in each series with collars of the facing colour which would otherwise look identical from a distance

when gloves were worn.[2] The shoulder-strap of the cuirass is well detailed, but the existence of only a single slot in the end designed to fit over the bolt protruding from the chest of the cuirass is almost unprecedented because it means that there was no way to adjust the fit of the breast and back plates.[3] The slotted piece should also end in a flexible leather tab. The sabre is also accurately depicted, but the upper reinforcing band (and belt ring) of the scabbard should be lower down.[4] The saddle covers and other tack are once again accurate only in broad outline and not in detail. All Cuirassier prints in the Martinet series show the white grenade ornament in the corner of the saddlecloth.

1   A close-up photograph of the helmet of trooper of the 4th Cuirassiers which features a Medusa head ornament in this location can be found on page 21 of Rigo, 'Les Cuirassiers'.
2   E.-L. Bucquoy, *Les Cuirassiers* (Paris 1976) is one of the few books in the series reproducing Bucquoy's famous uniform prints that has a thoughtful and scholarly text (which was originally published as a separate book in 1934). Plate No. 44 of that work by Benigni (p. 65) shows an NCO of the 6th Regiment with white collar trim in 1803, but there is no discussion of the sources for that painting.
3   See the discussion of cuirass models in Michel Pétard, 'Les Hommes de Fer', *Tradition* No. 54–55 (July/August 1991), pp. 40–46.
4   Michel Pétard, 'Le Sabre des Cuirassiers', *Tradition* No. 54–55 (July/August 1991), pp. 28–33.

Cuirassier

71
Cuirassier of the 9th Regiment

As noted previously, it is almost impossible to identify with certainty the regiment of any Cuirassier on the basis of his uniform alone if the relevant figure is wearing gloves which obscure the arrangement of facing colours on the cuff and cuff flap. In this case, however, the caption and the number on the portmanteau fit well with the yellow facings that are visible, and so seem to be reasonably reliable indicators that this figure is indeed a trooper of the 9th Cuirassiers. The figure has been drawn from a slightly different perspective from that of the preceding figure and provides a better sense of both the ridge running down the front of the breast plate and the black leather waist strap with buckle. The end of the cuirass shoulder-strap now has the typical two slots, but the leather tab is still missing.[1] The helmet is beautifully drawn and is consistent in all details with a surviving helmet of the regiment recovered from the battlefield of Essling except, again, the lack of ornamentation on the front edge of the crest.[2] The white plume, however, is extraordinary, because that item was, in theory at least, reserved for the exclusive use of members of the regimental staff. Rigo has theorized that it may have been worn more generally in the 9th to help distinguish their uniform from that of the similarly dressed 7th Regiment.[3] The sabre belt is much narrower than was the norm, and there is no shoulderbelt at all, a circumstance which suggests strongly that this trooper was not carrying a firearm. Once again, the details of the tack are roughly correct, but no other sources show a cylindrical portmanteau for any Cuirassier regiment even though that shape had been standard for heavy cavalry regiments from the promulgation of the cavalry equipment regulation of 1 April 1791 until the creation of the Cuirassier arm.[4] Some sources have asserted that the 9th Regiment retained the old-fashioned hair style with a queue until 1809, but there is obviously no sign of that feature in this painting.

1   One source suggests that the shoulder-strap for the 9th Regiment was always covered with chain mail rather than metal scales, but that is obviously not the case in this painting. J. Margerand, 'Le Centenaire des Cuirassiers [Pt. II]', *Carnet de la Sabretache* (1905), pp. 1–32, at 19.
2   R. and J. Brunon and Ch. Poher, 'Quatre Casques de Cuirassiers provenant d'Essling et de Wagram', *Uniformes* No. 46 (November/ December 1978), pp. 9–13, at 12.
3   *Le Plumet* Plate No. U 11: *Cuirassiers – 1er régiment en 1801, 9e en 1806–1808, 13e en 1813.*
4   MacCarthy, *La Cavalerie Française*, pp. 213, 246–252.

Cuirasfier du 9.me Regiment.

72
Trumpeter of the 9th Regiment of Cuirassiers

This singular figure poses a number of iconographic challenges because none of the most prominent features of his uniform comport with accepted information about the dress of Cuirassier trumpeters. Where one would expect to find a traditional reversed colour scheme featuring a yellow jacket accented with dark blue facings, this painting instead presents a colour scheme of buff/chamois and medium blue which is unprecedented for any Napoleonic uniform. There should be no question that we are seeing the exact shades intended by the Otto artist, because the preceding Plate clearly establishes that he had use of dark blue and yellow paints which have not faded over time. Both Rigo and Rousselot have, nevertheless, reproduced the colour of the jacket as a vivid yellow, and Rousselot compounds his error by adding a dark blue collar and turnbacks.[1] (Both artists have also added the missing numeral '9' on the end of the portmanteau.) There is no obvious explanation for the buff jacket, but there is authentic precedent for the facing colour in that Martinet Plate No. 240 illustrates a trumpeter of the 7th Cuirassiers in a yellow jacket with a medium blue collar and seated on a medium blue saddlecloth. The bearskin cap probably represents an effort to make use of the élite company head-dress inherited by the 9th from its constituent heavy cavalry regiments. It has a plain red backpatch encircled by a band of white lace, and metal chinscales which appear to be inaccurately depicted because they end at mid-cheek. This figure (in contrast to the preceding trooper) is wearing a cartridge box belt over the left shoulder. His shoulder-knots seem to have four instead of only three whorls, and there is a curious loop in the end of the shaft of the trumpet nearest to the mouth piece. This trumpeter is the first in the Manuscript to be riding a white horse. The size, shape and design of the sabre belt and belt plate are accurate, except that the raised edge around the latter item is unusual. The short tails and lack of lapels on this jacket seem to indicate that the painting illustrates the 'habit droit' style of coat identified by Bucquoy.[2] The harness is well detailed but fanciful, and there appears here for the first time the brown head stall which recurs in several other paintings, indicating that the Otto artist at least intended his depictions to be accurate.

1 See *Le Plumet* Plate No. 210: *Cuirassiers – 9e Régiment Trompettes 1807–1808* and Rousselot Plate No. 102: *Cuirassiers –Trompettes (II) 1804–1812.* There is, however, a possibility that there may have been other contemporary sources which show this same uniform with the more traditional colour scheme, although these cannot be traced today. See Comdt. Bucquoy's discussion of Rousselot's painting of a 9th Cuirassier trumpeter for his card series in Bucquoy, *Les Cuirassiers*, p. 139.

2 Bucquoy, *Les Cuirassiers*, pp. 57–59.

Trompette du 9ᵐᵉ Regiment des Cuirassiers

73
Officer of the 3rd Regiment of Dragoons

From the top of his helmet to the tip of his sabre, this officer is very elegantly turned-out, but in fact his uniform is quite unadventurous in the way in which it follows established patterns. The helmet is finely detailed down to the decorative work on the leading edge of its crest, but its most obvious highlight is the leopard skin turban around the base of the helmet with an extension on to the brass-trimmed brim.[1] Note also, however, the metal casing for the horsehair knot at the top of the crest and the suggestion of a Medusa's head ornament on the crest's leading edge. Rousselot has commented on the vast variety of Dragoon plume colour combinations shown in contemporary prints, but none of these corresponds to the relatively straightforward green tipped red example shown here.[2] Because neither the cuffs nor the pockets are visible, it is impossible to confirm for certain the attribution in the caption that he belongs to the 3rd Regiment, but the scarlet collar and lapels with green piping are consistent with that con-

clusion. The sidearm is an Otto gem in that it is a perfect representation of the lightly curved version of the standard Dragoon officer's model sabre, with a clearly identifiable scallop shell ornament worked into the guard and a black leather scabbard with three gilt metal reinforcements and two belt rings.[3] The saddlecloth and the round portmanteau are quite unusual because they represent patterns adopted in 1792 but discontinued in Year X, but the retention of out-dated items for campaign use was not at all unusual.[4] Dragoons were supposed to be clean-shaven, but this officer sports a full and somewhat sinister-looking moustache.

1 The overall effect is similar to that presented by an officer's helmet illustrated in Michel Pétard, 'Un Capitaine du 10e Dragons Vers 1808', *Tradition* No. 34 (Nov. 1989), pp. 38–45, at 42.
2 Rousselot Plate No. 7: *Dragons 1804–1815* (Paris 1943/1978).
3 Rousselot Plate No. 25: *Dragons – Officiers 1804–1815* (Paris 1943/1978). Compare this painting of the sabre with the photograph of a similar (albeit straight-bladed) sabre in Willing, Vol. II, p. 27.
4 E. Bucquoy, *Dragons et Guides* (Paris 1980), at 25 and 33.

Officier du 3me Regiment des Dragons.

74
Dragoon of the 3rd Regiment

In many ways the tremendous research value of the Otto Manuscript is most evident in the case of a painting like this one, which seems unexceptional at first glance, but which contains a wealth of uniform details that can be appreciated only on closer inspection. The easiest novelty to spot is the white plume with red top and bottom, but every element of the helmet from the knot of horsehair at the top of the crest (which, unlike that on the officer's helmet, has no metal casing) to the brass trim on the visor has been accurately rendered in a way that compares favourably with modern photographs of the same item.[1] As befits a Dragoon trooper without élite status, the shoulders of the uniform jacket are adorned only with cloth straps. As discussed in Plate No. 30 (Officer and Fusilier of the 8th Regiment) above, the placement of the button on the end of the strap away from the collar is noteworthy, but this feature is confirmed for this regiment in Martinet Plate No. 38: Cavalerie Légère, Dragon, 3e Régiment. The guard of the sabre, too, is unusual in that it does not resemble the standard three-branch model in general use during the First Empire, but it turns out that the Otto artist has in fact illustrated a sabre of the pattern introduced in Year IV in steel but which was later manufactured in brass versions.[2] This painting confirms the use by the Dragoons of a sheepskin saddlecloth (with decorative edging in the facing colour) flung over the regulation pistol holsters and leather saddle, but one might have expected the retaining strap to be black rather than white as shown here. The green cloth with the regimental number in the corner and the portmanteau with square end are both regulation, but the extra line of piping around the latter is not. Once again, the depiction of the harness is overly simplistic.[3]

1 See, e.g., the Dragoon helmet of the period 1806–1812 from a private collection which is illustrated by a photograph in *Fiche Technique* No. FDr 6 in *Uniformes* No. 77 (July/August 1983).
2 There is a close-up photograph of a hilt of this type in Rigo, 'Les Dragons en Egypte', *Tradition* No. 1 (January 1987), pp. 36–41, at 36.
3 A photograph of an existing example of Dragoon harness in the collections of the French Army Museum appears in Mac-Carthy, *La Cavalerie Française*, p. 258.

Dragon du 3ᵐᵉ Regiment.

75

Mounted Sapper of the
11th Regiment of Dragoons

This painting is one of the most significant in the Manuscript because there are very few authentic Napoleonic sources, written or iconographic, that confirm that Dragoon regiments did have Sappers just like Line and Light infantry regiments. Given that starting-point, the way this figure is dressed and equipped is predictable given the prominence of traditional Sapper features and effects. From an artistic viewpoint, however, the painting has some signal weaknesses which detract from its value. If the perspective of the bearskin is to be believed, the plume and raquette were positioned in the rear of the head-dress, an arrangement which seems highly improbable, and the chinscales are unrealistically positioned. Likewise, the ochre case for the head of the axe has been drawn at a peculiar angle to the location of the axe suggested by the appearance of the axe handle. (The case itself is interesting because there seems to be a second small case (perhaps a cartridge box) mounted on top.) Finally, the crossed-axes Sapper badge on the sleeve has been drawn in unreasonably small size which simply cannot be accurate. One point that is logically rendered is the apron with the skirt bunched at the rider's waist, because obviously the Sapper would have to devise some means of keeping the apron out of the way while he was on horseback. Note how the top of the apron extends over the lapels up to the bottom of the collar.

A less obvious problem with this painting is that the facings are not correct for the 11th Dragoons, because that regiment had crimson (and not scarlet, as shown here) for its distinctive colour and, in any event, was supposed to have green collars for its uniforms.[1] The white belt over the right shoulder has the correct dimensions for a Dragoon sabre belt, but this item of equipment was typically worn around the waist for mounted service. If this belt is the sabre belt, the purpose of the smaller ochre belt around the figure's waist becomes more problematical, although it may have been intended simply as a device to keep both the apron of untanned leather and the axe case in place. The saddle furnishings and harness have the same defects as in the preceding Plate, but one interesting feature is that the horseshoes have been accurately drawn.

---

1 Pétard, 'Le Dragon de Ligne', p. 22. Rousselot dealt with this discrepancy by dropping a number from the regimental designation and reproducing this figure as a Sapper of the 1st Dragoons, a unit which did have scarlet facings. See Figure 1 of Rousselot Plate No. 20: *Dragons – Sapeurs et Trompettes 1804–1815* (Paris 1943/1978).

Sappeur à cheval du 11.ms Regiment des Dragons.

76
Dragoons of the 20th and 6th Regiments

A. Dragoon of the 6th Regiment. The arrangement of facing colours on the collar, lapels and shoulder-strap piping of this figure is consistent with an attribution of this Dragoon to the 6th Regiment, but unfortunately the facing colour itself is not, a dull crimson/purple having been substituted for the regulation scarlet.[1] There is no obvious reason for this discrepancy except the possibility that the Otto artist this time made a mistake in the caption. The head-on view of the helmet reveals a serviceable if somewhat naïve attempt to depict the embossed metal Medusa's head and other decoration on the leading edge of the crest, but there is no sign of the shaped flanges extending at right angles from the base of the crest which permitted the crest to be screwed on to the top of the helmet.[2] The immense variety of Dragoon plume colours catalogued by Rousselot indicates that the use of a white plume was not particularly unusual.[3] This trooper is dressed for dismounted service, which means primarily that his sabre belt with brass buckle has been shifted from his waist to his right shoulder to create the crossed-belt appearance of most infantry figures, and he has been armed with a Dragoon-pattern musket with brass bands. The shoulder-straps (in this case with the button on the end near the collar) show that he belongs to a centre rather than an élite company. Another discrepancy is that the buttons of both the jacket and the vest are shown as being of brass rather than white metal.

B. Dragoon of the 20th Regiment. The problem in verifying the caption above this figure is a mirror image of that involved in identifying the other figure in the same painting – the yellow facing colour is correct for the 20th Dragoons (although one would have expected it to be a bit brighter), but the distribution of the colour is not, because the collar should be green.[4] (It is clear from other paintings in the Otto Manuscript that the artist had access to yellow pigments which have held their colour through time, but the yellow used in this painting has taken on an unfortunate brownish hue and is no longer the correct shade.) Visible between the legs of this figure is, presumably, the end of the sabre scabbard, but one would expect this piece of equipment to be black with a brass tip.

---

1 See Marchal, *Les Uniformes*, p. 21, and Martinet Plate No. 69: *Cavalerie Légère, Dragon, 6e Régiment.*
2 See, e.g., the photograph of an early Dragoon helmet taken from a similar perspective which is reproduced as *Fiche Technique* No. FDr 5 on the back cover of *Uniformes* No. 73 (March/April 1983).
3 Rousselot Plate No. 7.
4 Marchal, *Les Uniformes*, p. 23; Martinet Plate No. 109: *Cavalerie Légère, Dragon 20e Régiment.*

Dragon du
20ᵐᵉ Reg:

Dragon du
6ᵐᵉ Reg:

77

Hussar [Chasseur] of the 5th Regiment

The predominantly green colour of the uniform of this figure makes it certain that the caption is wrong and that the regiment depicted must in fact be the 5th Chasseurs, a unit which retained hussar-style uniforms with wing shakos long after they had been abandoned by other Chasseur regiments[1] and which was further distinguished by the use of buff leather belts and gloves.[2] Nevertheless, this identification is contradicted by the dirty ochre colour used for all the braid and lace. Even assuming that this colour was originally yellow, the designated facing colour for the 5th, an enigma exists because all other sources agree with the evidence of a contemporary painting by an officer of the regiment (which shows different ranks skirmishing with Cossacks in 1805 or 1807) that all uniform trim (other than that on the shoulder-straps) should have been white.[3] These facts leave little room for shades of interpretation – either the Otto artist was wrong or he observed a uniform variation that is otherwise unknown. In other respects, this painting and the Army Museum painting have many similarities. The shako in the latter painting is more cylindrical and lacks a cockade, but its buff-coloured 'wing', cords, plume and strip of white lace at the front are all identical. Both sources show a dolman with three vertical rows of white metal buttons and no sash, but the Otto garment is harder to identify as such because the dolman has been drawn unbuttoned to reveal the braided waistcoat beneath it. The Army Museum painting shows a button on the exterior portion of the shoulder-strap. The portmanteau and the sheepskin saddlecloth also match in both cases although, inconsistently, the '5' at the end of the Otto portmanteau is white. The Otto artist has made an effort to depict the intricacies of a light cavalry bridle and harness, but he succeeds only with respect to illustrating the standard method of carrying a carbine.

1   This head-dress, the name of which is derived from the reversible flap or wing of cloth which could be wrapped around the shako in different ways to produce a black or coloured result, was actually regulation for light cavalry in the early Consulate. Colonel Bonnemain of the 5th kept them in use for his unit long after they fell out of fashion because he personally felt they looked very smart. Rigo, 'Les Chasseurs à Cheval de la Ligne 1800–1814', *Tradition* No. 42–43 (July/August 1970), pp. 29–44, at 33.
2   The origins of this use of distinctive leatherwork remain unidentified. Rigo, 'Les Chasseurs à Cheval de la Ligne – 1er Époque 1801–1808', *Uniformes* No. 36 (March/April 1977), pp. 30–36 at 33.
3   The painting can be found in the French Army Museum in Paris, but it is reproduced on the cover of *Uniformes* No. 36 (March/April 1977).

Houssard du 5.me Regiment.

78

Grenadier [Elite Trooper] of the
24th Regiment of Mounted Chasseurs

This painting begins a series concerning the 24th Regiment of Chasseurs which is one of the most completely realized sequences in the Manuscript because it shows the uniforms of four different ranks within that unit. As evidenced by his fur busby and red epaulettes, this initial figure is a trooper of the élite company (the first company of the first squadron), and the style of his dress indicates that the 24th was one of the first Chasseur regiments to adopt the relatively modern-looking single-breasted coat with short tails known as the 'Kinski' jacket.[1] The designated colour of the 24th was capucine, which was certainly a shade of orange, but the facings in this painting seem very close to scarlet.[2] The busby is noteworthy for its cords (which were rarely worn other than by units of the Imperial Guard, perhaps because the busby bag could interfere with the way they hung) and for the fact that it provides another unrealistic depiction of chinscales by showing them as being plainly visible against the fur of the busby whereas they should be nestled out of sight. (One would have expected the chinscales themselves to have been of white metal instead of brass.) There are two shoulder-belts, one for the cartridge box and one for the carbine, and the uppermost belt has been decorated with a brass grenade ornament on a red cloth background. The uniform is completed by utilitarian green overalls with a double stripe down the side. Note the reinforcement of brown leather at the bottom of the trouser leg and the strap looping under the instep to hold the trousers in place. The sabre is a beautifully accurate rendering of the famous 'Montmorency' style of weapon, originally developed exclusively for the 2nd Chasseurs but which was widely used by all Chasseurs units from 1790 until the adoption of the newer Year XI model of sabre.[3] The sheepskin saddlecloth with capucine trim should probably extend under the portmanteau and should probably also have a black retaining strap instead of the white one shown.

1 The origins of this particular style have never been precisely identified. Rousselot Plate No. 11: *Chasseurs à Cheval – Généralités 1804–1814.*
2 See Plate No. 41 (Sapper of 25th Regiment) for a further discussion of the colour *capucine*. The facing colour depicted in Martinet Plate No. 66: *Chasseurs à Cheval, 24 Régiment* is decisively orange and decisively lighter in shade.
3 Two different perspectives of this weapon are illustrated by Rigo in paintings appearing in *Tradition* No. 42–43 (July/August 1990), at 37–38. A sabre of this type is also worn by a mannequin wearing the dress of the 8th Chasseurs which appears in the collections of the French Army Museum in Paris.

Grenadier du 24ᵐᵉ Regiment des Chasteur à ch

79

Trumpeter of the 24th Regiment of Mounted Chasseurs

The colour scheme of this uniform surely takes first prize for the most theatrical in the Manuscript and, indeed, there is little that might explain the appearance of this figure other than a sense of flamboyance on the part of the regimental commander. The 24th had been stationed in Italy for several years before being summoned to join the Grand Army early in 1807, and so apparently had greater scope for creative enhancement of its regimental image than units more directly under the scrutiny of the army bureaucracy.[1] The exact identification of the shade of red used in this painting once again presents difficulties, but the fact that the plume is darker than the rest of the red items leads one to conclude that the plume is plain red or scarlet and the jacket, trouser stripe and saddlecloth trim are all intended to be the facing colour, capucine. The use of sky-blue for the other items (instead of the green which would have been the obvious result of a 'reversed colours' approach) is, however, genuinely inexplicable. Given that this soldier is wearing a busby and a red plume, there is a possibility that he was a trumpeter of the élite company and that the other trumpeters of the regiment would have had a more traditional appearance. This figure has eschewed gauntlet gloves in favour of a lighter pair which would interfere less with the playing of his instrument, so the pointed cuff trimmed with white can be seen. The trefoil shoulder ornaments are similar to others depicted in the Manuscript except that the each of the loops is hollow and the one at the extremity of the shoulder is larger than the others. This trumpeter wears the same style of overalls as his élite company colleague, but has substituted one thick side stripe for the double stripe of the latter. The brown leather reinforcement at the bottom of the trouser leg shows up more clearly against this colour scheme. The portmanteau, which can be glimpsed behind the bell of the trumpet, is also sky-blue and has white trim, but there is no indication of a regimental number. The trumpeter is clean-shaven.

1   L. Picard, *La Cavalerie dans les Guerres de la Révolution et de L'Empire* (2 vols., Saumur 1895), p. 377.

Trompette du 24me Regiment des Chasseurs à cheval.

80
Officer of the 24th Regiment
of Mounted Chasseurs

The simple but significant contrasts between the uniform of an officer and the uniform of a trooper are abundantly apparent from a comparison of this painting with Plate No. 78. Following the principle of simplicity in dress put forward by Napoleon himself by virtue of his wearing the undress uniform of a Colonel of the Guard Chasseurs, this officer has chosen a busby with much less decoration than that of the trooper. The cut and colours of the jacket and trousers are identical in both cases, but the officer has only a single stripe on his trousers. He also wears a pair of silver epaulettes and the decoration of the Legion of Honour. The cartridge and sword belts both appear to be the same bright shade as the facings even though that would have been a difficult colour to produce by dyeing leather.[1] Given the colour of the regimental buttons, it is surprising to find that the belting has brass/gilt instead of silver metal fittings.[2] The sabre with shell guard looks more like a Dragoon's weapon than one for the light cavalry.

Officers typically did use a cloth saddlecover, but the trim and ornaments were most often silver rather the colour of the facings, and the hunting horn in this case seems unusually small.[3] The portmanteau is unusual because of the rings of red and green piping surrounding the normal ring of silver (?) lace and the absence of the regimental number. The artist has gone to considerable effort to show a red trim on the brown head stall, but the harness as a whole lacks the profusion of silver ornaments that one would expect for any self-respecting Chasseur officer.[4]

---

1   See, e.g., the darker red colour of the shoulder belt and cartridge box of an officer of the 2nd Hussars presented photographically in Bertrand Malvaux, 'Une Giberne d'Officier du 2e Hussards', *Tradition* No. 71 (December 1992), pp. 10–11.
2   The cartridge box itself would have been red with a silver hunting horn ornament with the number '24' in the middle. See Michel Pétard's painting of such an item belonging to an officer of the 24th which is now in the French Army Museum in Salon-de-Provence in *Équipements Militaires* Vol. IV, Pt. 1, p. 54.
3   Rousselot Plate No. 49: *Chasseurs à Cheval – Officiers 1804–1814*.
4   *Ibid*. See also, for example, Martinet Plate No. 189: *Officier de Chasseurs à Cheval, 2 Régiment, Compagnie d'Élite*.

81
[Trooper of the] 24th Regiment
of Mounted Chasseurs

The uniform of the Chasseur depicted in this painting mimics quite closely that of his élite company colleague. The expensive fur busby, however, has been replaced by a very simple model of shako which features an enlarged cockade as its only ornament. (The cockade's arrangement of colours differs from the norm.) The absence of a shako plate seems odd, but there are at least two other contemporary depictions of the 24th (one a Martinet Plate, the other a drawing by Albrecht Adam) which confirm this detail.[1] A red plume sported by this soldier is noteworthy, because such items were typically used only by élite companies, and so is the coloured pom-pom at its base.[2] There is a definite line of piping around the upper edge of the collar which does not appear in the Martinet Plate, but that source does show the same placement of the button for the shoulder-strap. The depiction of a vent pick attached by chain to one of the buttons on the front of the jacket shows that this tool was also used by mounted troops. The shoulder belts of this figure are held together by a modest double button, or stud, rather than the grenade ornament used by the élite company.[3] The end of the portmanteau has an extra inner ring of white trim. The breast strap of the harness has a heart-shaped ornament rather than the circular one found in the painting of the élite company trooper. On the evidence of battlefield relics, both styles were used by the 24th.[4]

1 See Martinet Plate No. 66: *Chasseurs à Cheval – 24e Régiment* and a drawing by Adam reproduced in Rigo and G. Englebert, 'Albrecht Adam et les Grognards (2e Partie)', *Uniformes* No. 96 (July/August 1986), p. 37.
2 Rigo asserts that this pom-pom is green, but to the naked eye it looks as if it might equally well be blue. *Le Plumet* Plate No. U6: *Chasseurs à Cheval, Sapeur du 13e Régiment, Cavaliers du 24e 1808–1809*. He goes on to conclude that a green pom-pom signifies a member of the 4th Squadron, which did not join the Regiment in Germany until 1808, but that claim is based solely on a description of the pom-pom colours of the 15th Chasseurs in August 1814, after the first restoration of the Bourbons. A.D., 'Extraits du Livre d'Ordres du 15e Régiment de Chasseurs 1812–1814', *Carnet de la Sabretache* (1930), pp. 289–293.
3 This arrangement is the subject of a detailed drawing by Rigo in 'Les Hussards du Premier Consul', *Tradition* No. 66–67 (July/August 1992), pp. 30–40, at 33–34.
4 Georges Englebert, 'Objets Militaires Retrouvés à Essling et Wagram', *Uniformes* No. 59 (January/February 1981), pp. 27–30, at 28.

24ᵐᵉ Regiment des Chasseurs à cheval

82
Grenadier [Elite Trooper] of the 26th Regiment of Mounted Chasseurs

This figure is wearing the most traditional (and most common) Chasseur uniform of the First Empire, which evolved from the replacement of the dolman by a long-tailed jacket with lapels. Despite the evidence of the caption, the breast ornament on the harness and the end of the portmanteau, there is doubt about the assignment of this figure to the 26th Chasseurs for two reasons. First, the distinctive colour on this uniform is a bright orange which seems identical with the capucine facings worn by the preceding figure, yet the facings of the 26th were supposed to be madder red, a moderate to strong shade which would be much darker.[1] Secondly, the 26th was supposed to have its facing colour only on the cuffs, and not on the collars, of its uniforms, which is certainly not the case here. Of the possible explanations for these peculiarities, the most persuasive is that the Otto artist has in fact depicted a trooper of the 22nd Chasseurs, a unit which was distinguished by capucine collars and cuffs (with green trim)[2] and which, coincidentally, served briefly in the same brigade as the 26th during the winter of 1807, which wore the same style of uniform.[3] The élite status of this trooper is once again evidenced by the use of epaulettes (in this case white instead of the traditional red) and of a fur busby with scarlet plume and bag and white cords. The green waistcoat with white braid was a common uniform feature, but coloured and plain waistcoats were also worn.[4] The Hungarian-style breeches have a typical arrangement of lace outlining the seams of the front flap and the outside of the leg. Given the profusion of trim on this uniform, it is surprising to find no lace around the top of the boots. The perspective allows a clear view of the Year IX model musketoon.[5]

1   Marchal, *Les Uniformes*, p. 30.
2   *Ibid.*, p. 29.
3   The use of this style of uniform by the 22nd is confirmed by a contemporary painting reproduced in E.M., 'Portrait d'un Sous-Officier du 22e Régiment de Chasseurs à Cheval (1810)', *Carnet de la Sabretache* (1907).
4   L. Bernadin, 'Les Chasseurs à Cheval 1800–1814', *La Giberne* Vol. 6 (1904-05), pp. 145–165, at 155.
5   Laurent Mirouze, 'Le Mousqueton de Cavalerie An IX', *Tradition* No. 12 (January 1988), pp. 37–41; No. 14 (March 1988), pp. 28–33; and No. 28 (May 1989), pp. 6–7.

Grenadier du 26.me Regiment des Chasseur à Cheval.

83
Hussar of the 2nd Regiment

This painting provides another opportunity to verify the accuracy of the work of the Otto artist by comparison with an exceptional contemporary source, in this case a trio of watercolours in the collections of the French Army Museum drawn by Colonel Jean-François-Thérèse Barbier, who commanded the 2nd from 1793 to 1806. In the earliest of these pictures (showing the Staff of the unit in 1803-5), the only private soldier depicted is wearing a shako similar to that shown here which is decorated with an enlarged cockade (with a red outer ring) instead of a plate and a black plume.[1] The head-dress in the Otto painting still has unique elements, however, such as the spherical pom-pom divided vertically between white and red[2] and the wearing of brass chinscales by a unit which otherwise had white metal fittings. The brown pelisse is peculiar in a number of respects. First, it is closed down the front without pelisse cords, thereby leaving visible the black fur trim. (Compare this 'look' with that of the pelisse-clad troopers in the next two Plates.) Secondly, the pelisse has shoulder-straps, a feature rarely seen on this item of clothing. Finally, the braid seems to be mixed white and grey (?) in colour (and not merely white braid with heavy shading).[3] The plain black sabretache with brass ornament is highly unusual for the period,[4] but both it and the grey overalls with buttons and leather cuff are identical with those depicted by Barbier in one of his paintings.[5] The sabre shown represents the model with three-branch guard introduced in 1802.[6]

1 This picture is reproduced in Rigo, 'Hussards 2e Époque', *Uniformes* No. 33 (September/October 1976), pp. 6–16, p. 16.
2 This pom-pom may indicate membership in the second company of the first squadron since the first (élite) company in that formation indisputably wore a red pom-pom. *Ibid.* at 14–16.
3 Based on this detail, Rigo asserts that this pelisse may have been captured from the Prussians, although he cites no examples of Prussian hussars with variegated braid. See *Le Plumet* Plate No. U4: *Hussards – 2e Régiment 1803 et 1807.*
4 See Bertrand Malvaux, 'Les Sabretaches des Hussards', *Tradition* No. 65–66 (July/August 1992), pp. 22–29.
5 The painting, which has been dated to 1807, is reproduced in Alan Pigeard, 'A La Hussarde', *Tradition* No. 66–67 (July/August 1992), pp. 17–21, at 18. See also Cmdt. Bucquoy, *La Cavalerie Légère* (Paris 1980), p. 101.
6 Photographs of such sabres are reproduced in Michel Pétard, 'Les Sabres de Cavalerie Légère Mle. An IX-An XI', *Tradition* No. 65 (June 1992), pp. 4–9.

Houssard du 2.me Regiment.

84

Grenadier [Elite Trooper of the 5th Regiment] of Hussars

Although the caption does not identify the regiment to which this figure belongs, there is no mistaking the white pelisse of the 5th Hussars. The following is a full description of the regimental uniform in 1807, written by an officer who adjudged it 'the most elegant and magnificent' in the Grand Army:[1]

'... white pelisse with yellow wool lace, trim, cords and braid and black fur trim; sky-blue dolman and breeches decorated with yellow wool lace, braid and fringe; red vest with yellow lace and trim ... white sabretache trimmed with a wide band of lace and decorated with a brass eagle over the number "5"; curved sabre with brass scabbard; busby with white bag and brass chinscales ... The horse furniture consists of a hussar saddle ... sky-blue saddlecloth with yellow lace, a round sky-blue portmanteau with yellow lace on the ends; a brass heart on the breast harness, bridles decorated with brass and a bit without a boss.'

The uniform depicted in this painting conforms closely to this description, with both obvious (colour of the busby bag) and subtle (colour of the sabre scabbard) differences. Perhaps the most surprising aspect of the appearance of the Otto figure is that the sabre-tache has been entirely omitted, perhaps an indication that these expensive items of equipment were stored away for all but 'full dress' occasions. The spearhead decoration on the thigh of the breeches was probably the most common style employed by Hussars in the Grand Army, but trefoil and (so-called) 'Hungarian knot' patterns of lace were also used.[2] The pelisse should have a fourth vertical row of buttons on the other side of the central opening, but it does have the bit of scarlet ribbon indicating membership of the Legion of Honour. The sheepskin saddle cover with sky-blue trim is more appropriate for a trooper than the cloth version described by d'Espinchal, although, as usual, its dimensions have been mis-drawn[3] and the retaining strap across the front is shown as being white instead of black.

1 Hippolyte d'Espinchal, *Souvenirs Militaires (1792–1814)* (2 vols., Paris 1901), Vol. 1, p. 155.
2 A chart showing the variants for this feature used by the different Hussar regiments is provided in Rigo, 'Les Tribulations du Costume Militaires: Les Hussards – Troisième Époque, Le Premier Empire et L'Épopée', *Uniformes* No. 34 (November/December 1976), pp. 28–33, at 29–30.
3 See, by way of contrast, the detailed painting of saddle furniture and harness for a trooper of the 5th in *Le Plumet* Plate No. U13: *Hussards – 5e Régiment 1803–1806 et 1812*.

85
Grenadier [Elite Trooper of the 7th (?) Regiment] of Hussars

Because the caption to this painting lacks a specific unit designation, identifying the regiment to which this figure belongs is a difficult task because two regiments of Napoleonic Hussars had green and red uniforms – the 7th and the 8th. According to regulations, the only way they could be distinguished was by their lace and trim, which was supposed to be yellow (with brass buttons) for the 7th and white (with white metal buttons) for the 8th.[1] In practice, however, it seems that the 8th Hussars often wore red or mixed red and green braid on their pelisses and dolmans.[2] What the Otto artist appears to have seen, therefore, is either a trooper of the 7th Hussars wearing a pelisse belonging to the 8th Hussars (and using a portmanteau from the 8th as well), or a trooper of the 8th Hussars wearing the yellow-trimmed breeches and busby of a member of the 7th Hussars.[3] (Both these combinations are conceivable given the supply difficulties which faced most French regiments during the campaigns in Poland.) The mystery might be cleared up if this figure were wearing a sabretache bearing a regimental number or pattern, but in the absence of such a distinguishing item no definitive conclusion can be reached. On the whole, however, it seems slightly more plausible to identify this soldier as being a member of the 7th Hussars, there being no evidence of the use of yellow lace by the 8th Regiment cited in the detailed study of the dress of that unit conducted by Commandant Bucquoy.[4] No matter which unit is depicted, however, it is noteworthy that the pelisse has only three vertical rows of buttons and that, once again, there is no trim around the tops of the hussar-style boots.

1 Marchal, *Les Uniformes*, pp. 32–33. The source quoted by Marchal actually reports green breeches for the 8th, but that appears to have been a mistake. See Albert Depreaux, 'Le 8e Régiment de hussards et ses Officiers à L'époque du Consulat', *Carnet de la Sabretache* (1912), pp. 112–127, at p. 125, n. 1.
2 For instance, an observer in 1809 reports that the uniform of the 8th Hussars 'was bottle green with white buttons and variegated red and green braid, black fur, red breeches and shako. The officers as well as members of the élite company wore a bearskin busby.' Dumonceau, *Mémoires*, Vol. 1, p. 284.
3 Rigo assumes that the figure belongs to the 8th Hussars and ignores the yellow lace except to note that it is an oddity. *Le Plumet* Plate No. U24: *Hussards – 8e Régiment 1803 a 1814.*
4 The 24 Bucquoy cards relating to the 8th Hussars are reproduced in E. Bucquoy, *La Cavalerie Légère* (Paris 1980), pp. 48–61.

Grenadier des Houssares.

PART V
ARTILLERY AND SUPPORT TROOPS

PART V
ARTILLERY AND SUPPORT TROOPS

Like any complex social organization, the Grand Army also had many specialist troops which performed combatant and non-combatant functions complementary to the more straightforward tasks performed by its cavalry and infantry forces. The most important and numerous of these were the component units of the Corps of Artillery, an organization which, as in many countries during this period, was an autonomous branch of the armed forces. According to a Consular decision dated 10 October 1801 (which set out the basic organization of the Corps that was retained during the whole of Napoleon's reign), these components were line Foot Artillery,[1] Guard and line Horse Artillery, pontoniers, artillery artisans, the Artillery Train, veteran units and Coastal Artillery.[2]

Having trained as an artillery officer, Napoleon was keenly aware of the value of heavy guns on the battlefield and always attempted to have a relatively large number of cannon attached to his armies. As he wrote to his step-son Prince Eugène, 'The big battles are won with artillery.'[3] The Foot Artillery consisted of eight line regiments, each divided into twenty companies (or batteries) having an establishment of six to eight guns and 100 men.[4] The Foot Artillery uniform was of the same style as that of the line infantry, but with blue lapels and red cuffs and piping.[5] Horse Artillery units had become established in the French Army only since the Revolution,[6] but by 1807 there were six mounted line regi-

ments, each divided into six companies (or batteries) of 6–8 cannon each. The Horse Artillery had an elaborate blue and red Hussar-style uniform for full dress, but most often on campaign the men wore a less elaborate undress uniform:[7] '[national blue] surtout, red cuffs and trim, pointed lapels; [national blue] Hungarian breeches trimmed with red lace, blue greatcoat, Hungarian boots; shakos for headwear'.

By 1806 there were a full twenty battalions of Artillery Train (of six companies each).[8] Each Train company boasted close to 100 officers and men, who were in charge of a wide variety of wheeled transport ranging from ammunition caissons to portable forges. The uniform of the Artillery Train is set out in its organizational decree:[9]

'Jacket of iron grey cloth ... with national blue lapels and cuffs and the edges of the coat tails turned back and hooked into place, white metal buttons of the same model adopted for the artillery. Iron grey waistcoat with sleeves. Skin breeches.'

This iron grey distinctive of the Artillery Train was not in fact a grey colour at all, but a distinctly blue shade created by the weaving together of blue and white thread in the same cloth rather than by the use of dyes.

Another autonomous service was the Corps of Engineers, which had been detached from the Artillery in 1793 as one of the reforms of the Revolution. In most cases Engineer officers were expected to carry out their duties of building and repairing fortifications, and capturing those of the enemy, with whatever manpower happened to be available. Nevertheless, the Corps also had its own skilled labour force distributed throughout the Grand Army so that, in theory at least, there was always a cadre of trained men to work on any engineering project. By 1807, this force consisted of five battalions of Sappers, nine companies of Miners, and related baggage train and security formations. Each Sapper battalion was comprised of nine companies of eighty men each, while each company of Miners fielded 100 men on a war footing.[10] The uniform of the Engineers was similar to that of artillerymen, except that all the facings were black instead of blue.

The last formation of particular significance was the Corps of Imperial Gendarmes which served as the national police of France. In wartime, the Corps was called upon to provide Gendarmes for service with the Grand Army both in specific units assigned to the headquarters of the Grand Army and of each of its constituent corps and in small detachments spread out along the French lines of communications.[11] Their primary function was that of any modern military police – the maintenance of public order in rear echelon areas.

The army also fielded a variety of other specialist services, none of which is represented in the Otto Manuscript. These were both of combatant and non-combatant types, including the Baggage Train, Medical Corps, Postal Service and a variety of logistical services.

1   Artillerymen were divided into horse and foot units depending whether the gunners rode or walked alongside their weapons.
2   *Organisation Militaire des Armées Françaises de 1791 à 1815* (Paris n.d. [1900]), p. 81. See also Détaille, E. and Richard, J., *L'Armée Française – An Illustrated History of the French Army, 1790–1885* (New York 1992), p. 235. (This work is an English translation of the French work published in 1885.)
3   Napoleon to Eugène, 20 November 1813, *Correspondance*, Vol. 26, No. 20929.
4   Alombert & Colin, Vol. 1, p. 131.
5   Rousselot Plate No. 28: *Artillerie à Pied 1804–1815* (Paris 1943/1978).
6   Matti Lauerma, *L'Artillerie de Campagne Française Pendant les Guerres de la Révolution – Évolution de L'Organisation et de la Tactique* (Helsinki 1956), pp. 98–101.
7   Marchal, *Les Uniformes*, pp. 34–35.
8   The battalions were numbered 1 to 10 and 1 *bis* [1 Alternate] to 10 *bis*. *Le Plumet* Plate No. U17: *Train d'artillerie – 1er Bataillon bis; Artillerie à Cheval – 3e Régiment 1807–1808.*
9   Order of 16 Thermidor Year 9 [4 August 1801], *Journal Militaire* for Year IX [1801], Part 2, p. 556–558.
10 Alombert & Colin, Vol. 1, pp. 128–129.
11 A total of 538 Gendarmes were on active service as of 7 October 1806. G. Lechartier, *Les Services de L'Arrière à la Grande Armée en 1806–1807* (Paris 1910), p. 207–208.

86
Horse Artillery

From a modern perspective, the campaign uniform of the French Horse Artillery of the Line is only slightly less impressive than the hussar-style costume worn on full dress occasions.[1] Indeed, the two states of dress are quite similar, the only differences being the substitution of the jacket with pointed lapels and the braided waistcoat shown in this painting for the regulation dolman and sash and the elimination of the sabretache.[2] The Horse Artillery also seem to have observed the dress regulations quite closely, because the uniform depicted here is practically identical with those depicted in Zimmerman drawing No. 24: Artillerie à Cheval and Weiland's print of a Canonnier à Cheval. If further evidence of the accuracy of this painting is needed, it is provided by a comparison of this figure's head-dress with the shako of the 3rd Artillery Regiment in the French Army Museum.[3] Once again, the details of the Otto version are confirmed by the authentic artefact, although the grenade ornament on the museum piece has inscribed on it the regimental number '3'. The only jarring note in this picture is the white colour of the numeral on the end of the portmanteau. Given the predominance of the colour red for all other ornamentation and trim, this detail is certainly suspect. The sabre with single guard is, on the other hand, exceptionally well-drawn.[4]

1 For a depiction of the full dress uniform, see Martinet Plate No. 60: *Canonnier à Cheval*.
2 See Rousselot Plate No. 36: *Artillerie à Cheval* (Paris 1943/1978), Michel Pétard, 'L'Homme de 1807 – Le Canonnier à Cheval', *Uniformes* No. 43 (May/June 1978), pp. 22–28.
3 See Willing, Vol. 1, p. 97.
4 Michel Pétard, 'Les Sabres "Allemand' et "Hongroise" des Hussards', *Tradition* No. 66–67 (July/August 1992), pp. 8–16.

Artillerie à cheval

87
Foot Artillery [1st Battalion of Sappers]

A. First Class Sapper. The predominantly blue and red colours of the uniform of the two figures in this painting certainly suggests a connection with the artillery service, but the undeniably black collar, lapels, cuffs and cuff flaps make it certain that the caption for this painting is wrong and that the figures represented are actually Sappers, one of the two types of specialist troops (the other being Miners) making up the French Corps of Military Engineers.[1] This conclusion is reinforced by the design of the shako plate, which is similar to that of a surviving plate from the 3rd Company of Miners, although that artefact has a device rather than a numeral in the central medallion.[2] The numeral in the medallion in this painting suggests for obvious reasons that this Sapper may be a member of the 1st Sapper Battalion. The personnel of each Sapper company was divided on the basis of seniority into first and second class Sappers. This figure cane be identified as a 1st Class Sapper because of his red epaulettes.[3]

B. Second Class Sapper. The replacement of the epaulettes of the first figure with the black shoulder-straps with red trim indicate that this figure is a 2nd Class Sapper.[4] Except for this one difference, his uniform is identical with that of the first figure in this painting and with that of another Sapper illustrated in the so-called Ornstrup Manuscript.[5] Because all Sappers were considered to have élite status, this figure also carries a sabre just like that of his first class colleague.

1 This identification is also made by Rigo in *Le Plumet* Plate No. U28: *Genie – 1er et 5e Batallions de Sapeurs 1801–1808.* The plate contains a brief history of the battalion.
2 Blondieau, *Aigles et Shakos*, p. 20. Surprisingly, although Rigo purports to reproduce this shako plate as a detail in *Le Plumet* No. U28, he incorrectly depicts the base as bearing the name of the unit.
3 At least one source shows Sapper epaulettes as having been yellow during the Revolution, but they certainly had become red by the start of the Imperial era. Roger Forthoffer, *Fiche Documentaire* No. 245: *France – Le Génie 1792–1815.*
4 Rigo, '1804, Le 5e Batallion du Gènie. . . ou des Bras de Fer dans les Parements de Velours', *Tradition* No. 49 (February 1991), pp. 10–15, p. 14.
5 For more information about this source, consult Note 23 and accompanying text in Part I above.

enadier. *Artillerie à pied*

88
Soldier and Officer of the Artillery Train

A. Soldier. This painting provides confirmation of two important pieces of information about the dress of the Artillery Train of the line, which wore a uniform identical with that of the Guard Train except for the absence of red trim. First, the official uniform regulations for that service make no mention of the colour of the collar, but all sources agree with the evidence of this painting that the collar was also blue.[1] Secondly, this painting resolves the question of whether Artillery Train lapels were pointed or square. The Artillery Train originally wore bicorne hats, but shakos came to be worn with such frequency that Napoleon ultimately ruled that they were to be the regulation head-dress.[2] The one depicted here is quite elaborate, with cords of iron grey (or, according to Rigo, mixed iron grey and white), a shako plate with a rectangular base and a visor with metal trim and unusual squared edges. It also has a circular pom-pom bearing the numeral '1' (which was probably originally white), which numeral also appears below the crossed cannon on the belt plate and on the end of the small trunk by his foot.[3]

The belt plate differs from surviving examples in having raised white metal trim around its edge. The sabre baldric is accurately shown, but the connection to the sabre should consist of one thick leather piece rather than the two thin strips shown here.[4]

B. Officer. The white plume on this officer's shako would be surprising except that all Wagon Train officers were deemed to be part of the battalion staff. The rest of his rank distinctions are similar to those that have been seen elsewhere in the Otto Manuscript, but they make for a particularly striking ensemble in this case.

---

1 See generally, Rousselot Plate No. 55: *Train d'artillerie 1801–1814* (Paris 1979), and Michel Pétard, 'L'Homme de 1808 – Le Train d'artillerie', *Uniformes* No. 64 (November/December 1981), pp. 23–30.
2 Napoleon I, *Ordres et Apostilles de Napoléon* (4 Vols., Paris 1911–12) (A. Chuquet, ed.), Item No. 3661 (12 August 1807), Vol. 3, p. 167.
3 Rigo asserts without explanation that this figure actually belongs to the 4th company of Train Battalion 1 bis. See *Le Plumet* Plate No. U17: *Train d'artillerie – 1er Batallion bis; Artillerie à Cheval – 3e régiment 1807–1808.*
4 Pétard, *Équipements Militaires*, Vol. 4, Pt. 1, p. 58.

Soldat des Trains d'Artillerie.   Officier.

89
Gendarme

The decisive elements in the identification of this figure as a member of the Imperial Gendarmerie are the large bicorne with a wide band of white lace and the white aiguillette on the left shoulder.[1] Other contemporary illustrations of Gendarmes in Zimmerman Drawing No. 32, Martinet Plate No. 21 and Weiland confirm these details although they all show the full dress blue uniform with signature red lapels rather than the single-breasted campaign jacket. They, together with this painting, also provide compelling evidence to support the conclusion that mounted Gendarmes routinely wore a white trefoil ornament on the right shoulder to complement the trefoil and aiguillette on the left shoulder even though this was not officially sanctioned.[2] There is a painting in the Hamburg Manuscript (Plate No. 42) of three Gendarmes of the 8th Corps in surtouts which confirms both the detail of the red trim on the collar (but not elsewhere) and the fact that the aiguillette had four strands of cord. On the other hand, the figures in the Hamburg painting have no ornamentation at all on their right shoulders. The buff gloves and breeches are typical for Gendarmes, although the shade of the trousers seems darker than might be expected. The double shoulder-belt indicates that this Gendarme must have carried a firearm on the side away from the viewer. The sabre has a very unusual medallion worked into the guard of its hilt. The horse furniture is, as usual, somewhat inaccurately drawn, but seems to be correct as to colour and ornaments.[3]

1 The basic dress of the Gendarmes during the First Empire was derived from a 1799 law which is reproduced in La Grenadiere, 'Uniforme de la Gendarmerie Nationale (Loi de 28 Germinal, An 7 (17 Avril 1799))', *La Giberne* Vol. 6 (1904–1905), pp. 7–8, 23–24, 38–40, 55–58, 72–74 and 105–106. See also the description of Gendarme uniforms in E. Martin, *La Gendarmerie en Espagne et en Portugal* (Paris 1898), pp. 26–31.
2 See the detailed painting of an aiguillette and matching right side trefle epaulette in E. L. Bucquoy, 'Souvenirs de la Gendarmerie Impériale', *Le Passepoil* Vol. 3 (1923), pp. 49–52 and Plate 7, at p. 51. This pattern of ornamentation was definitely worn by the Élite Gendarmes of the Imperial Guard. See generally, Michel Pétard 'L'Homme de 1806 – Le Gendarme d'Élite de la Garde', *Uniformes* No. 90 (September/October 1985).
3 See Rousselot Plate No. 61: *Gendarmerie Nationale 1791–1800* (Paris 1958/1982).

Gens d'armes.

PART VI
ITALIAN TROOPS

PART VI
ITALIAN TROOPS

Although it is well-known that Napoleon was the King of Italy as well as the Emperor of the French, it is less well-known that Italian troops, which played such a prominent role in the Austrian War of 1809 and the Russian War of 1812, also participated in some of the subsidiary operations of the 1807 Campaign.[1] The first Italian contingent called on in this regard by Napoleon consisted of the First Line Regiment, the 1st and 2nd Light Regiments and a company of Sappers, all of whom had been part of an auxiliary division of Italian troops stationed on the coasts of the English Channel. These troops reached Germany at the beginning of 1807 and were added to the forces engaged in the siege of Colberg. During May and June of that same year, the Italians were joined by successive contingents of reinforcements consisting of new units and elements drawn from the depots of the formations already present in the North German theatre of war.

As might be expected, the organization and uniforms of the forces of the Kingdom of Italy had many similarities to those of the French Army of the same period. Overall, the Italian Army consisted in 1807 of the following components:[2]

Royal Guard
6 Line Infantry Regiments
2 Light Infantry Regiments
1 Dalmatian Regiment
1 battalion of Foot Chasseurs

2 regiments of Dragoons
2 regiments of Mounted Chasseurs
Foot Artillery
Horse Artillery
Artillery Train
Sappers
Gendarmes
Veterans
Sailors

The Italian infantry units that served with the Grand Army all had the same number of companies (with the same titles) as the comparable formations in the French armed forces. The foundation colour of their uniforms was green, the colour that had been adopted for the troops of the Cisalpine Republic.[3] The precise combinations of facings and features for the various units were apparently worked out in 1801–2, but exact information about Italian uniforms prior to the adoption of the 1807 Regulations is not easy to obtain.[4] The soldiers of the line regiments wore white vests and breeches, and green jackets whose white lapels had squared bottoms, and red collar and cuffs. The soldiers of the light regiments wore yellow vests and green breeches and had yellow collars and cuffs and green lapels (piped yellow) with tapered bottoms to their green jackets.[5] In theory, there were no regimental differences in light or line infantry dress other than the numbers on the buttons, but there were distinctions among the various types of companies within each unit which were identical (for the most part) with the corresponding distinctions in the French Army.

1   Bernard Druene, 'Les Debuts des Italiens à la Grande Armée 1806–1808', *Revue Historique de L'Armée* Vol. 29 (1973), No. 3, pp. 22–47.
2   Richard Knötel, 'Kurze Uebersicht uber die Formationen der Cisalpinisch-Italienischen Armee 1796–1814', *Mittheilungen zur Geschichte der Militarischen Tracht* Vol. 3, Nos. 4 (April 1892) and 5 (May 1892). A more detailed analysis of the organization of the Italian army is presented in Alessandro Zanoli's *Sulla Milizia Cisalpino-Italiano cenni Storico-statistici dal 1796 al 1814* (2 Vols., Milan 1845), Vol. 1, pp. 1–20.

3   See generally, Massimo Brandani, Piero Crociani and Massimo Fiorentino, *Uniformi Militari Italiane dell'Ottocento: Periodo Napoleonico* (Rome 1978), pp. 15–29. On 1 July 1807 a comprehensive new set of uniform regulations (the '1807 Regulations') was adopted by Viceroy Eugène Beauharnais which changed the base colour to white.
4   The only books which deal explicitly with Italian military dress of this early period are two privately printed works by a French researcher who has done an extraordinary job of compiling and analysing all available sources. See Jean-Pierre Perconte, *L'Infanterie Légère Italienne (1799–1814)* (n.l. n.d.) and *L'Infanterie de Ligne Italienne (1799–1814)* (hereinafter referred to as 'Perconte, *Infanterie Légère Italienne*' and 'Perconte, *Infanterie de Ligne Italienne*').
5   This colour scheme is shown consistently in Weiland's Plates of a '*Carabinier Italien*' and of an '*Officier des Chasseurs Italiens.*'

90
Sapper of the 1st Italian [Line] Regiment

This Plate presents more strong evidence concerning the reliability of the Otto Manuscript because the dress of this Sapper is nearly, but not exactly, identical with the dress of the Italian Sapper shown in the Hamburg Manuscript's Plate No. 34: Officier & Sapeur der Grenadier. The outstanding feature of his uniform is, without question, his magnificent white bearskin cap. This item must have been very expensive and it also must have been very difficult to care for on campaign. The arrangement of the bag and the cords is somewhat mystifying, but it seems that one of the raquettes on the right side is descending from the bag and the other is descending from the cords. (The arrangement is different in the Hamburg Plate.) The cockade under the plume should have a green centre, but its colour in this painting is too dark to be identified for certain. The use of the same white colour for the uniform jacket was quite unusual for an Italian soldier although during the course of 1807 the foundation colour of all Italian line infantry uniforms was changed to white. Also unusual is the single-breasted style

of the jacket, but the red epaulettes and the red Sapper arm badges are, of course, routine. The final points of interest in this painting are the light brown gloves and apron, and the black cartridge box worn at the waist suspended from a black belt. (In the Hamburg Plate, the apron covers the chest of the Sapper and has red piping around the edge and red grenades in its upper corners.) This Sapper sports the most patriarchal example of beard to be found in the Manuscript.

This painting and that of the Light Infantry Sapper in Plate No. 93 below are different stylistically from all the other Otto paintings. The subject is posed directly facing the viewer and the background is fully delineated. The figure even appears to be of a somewhat larger scale than the other paintings. Such circumstances might ordinarily lead to questions about the attribution of the painting, but in this case the odd perspective which allows the bottom of the stock of the Sapper's musket to be visible confirms that the Plate is the work of the Otto artist.

91
Officer and Grenadier of the 1st Italian Line Regiment

A. Officer. Although the dress of this officer clearly owes much to French style precedent, there are a number of ways in which it strikes out in unique directions. Starting with the head-dress, one must note the double cords which rise from left to right rather than from right to left, and which are also unusual in that one cord is significantly thicker than the other. The gold colour of the cords and the grenade plate (as well as of the gorget, epaulettes and belt buckle) is unexpected, because typically the metallic colour of officers' distinctions was based on the colour of the regimental buttons.[1] The coloured collar and cuffs (with cuff flaps as well) are relatively elaborate features for a single-breasted campaign surtout. (The absence of white piping along the top of the collar is probably an error by the artist.) Another oddity is the white turnbacks. In contrast to this figure is the depiction of an Italian Grenadier officer in campaign dress which can be found in the Hamburg Manuscript, who is wearing a bicorne hat, a green surtout with red collar and green cuffs, silver epaulettes and gorget, and green breeches.

B. Grenadier. A quick comparison of this soldier with the French Grenadier in Plate No. 39 shows that the style of uniform worn by the two figures is almost identical. This figure does have the same unusual configuration for the cords of his bearskin as does his officer, but otherwise only differences of jacket and button colour set the French and the Italian Grenadier apart. The musket of the latter is somewhat different, however, in that it has brass instead of silver bands. More perplexing issues arise from a further comparison of this soldier with the two Grenadiers illustrated in Hamburg Manuscript Plate No. 34 – Grenadiere. The latter are plainly members of the army of the Kingdom of Italy, because they also have green jackets and white lapels, and they also seem to belong to the First Line because one has the letter 'R' and the numeral '1' on each side of the grenade on the cap plate of his bearskin. In addition to this distinguishing feature, the figures in the Hamburg plate have green cuffs and, apparently, red turnbacks. They also lack piping on their collars.

---

1   The use of gold distinctions by Italian Line officers is also shown in Plate No. 45: Italian Officer of Grenadiers 2nd. Regt., of Infantry of the Line in *The Military Costume of Europe* published by T. Goddard and J. Booth (London n.d. [1812–1822]).

premier régiment
italienne de ligne

Officier   Grenadier

92
Officer and Voltigeur of the
First Italian [Line] Regiment

A. Officer. The schizophrenic approach to officers' distinctions noted in the previous Plate is here carried to its logical and absurd end, the massive amount of silver decoration on the shako of this officer contrasting markedly with the gold of his other badges of rank. The shako plate confirms the regimental designation from the caption because it is decorated with a Roman numeral 'I' surmounted by the iron crown of Lombardy, the chosen symbol of Napoleon's reign. The shako also sports a relatively large cockade, which differed from that of the French Army through the substitution of green for blue in the centre. It is unclear whether the original colour of the collar was buff or a yellow that has darkened with age, but the evidence of subsequent paintings of Italian soldiers suggests that the Otto artist was using a less stable yellow pigment for this section of the Manuscript than elsewhere. The detailing of the jacket cuff is as elaborate as for the preceding officer and, again, the lining of the coat tails is white. This figure is the only Voltigeur or light infantry officer in the Manuscript who is wearing a hunting horn device on his gorget. He also appears to be wearing the decoration of the Legion of Honour rather than some Italian decoration.

B. Voltigeur. The distinctions for the uniform of this Voltigeur obviously follow the French pattern, because he has a yellow collar, green shako cords, green epaulettes with a yellow crescent and a green sabre knot with yellow accent. The mound-shaped pom-pom on the shako is a different design from any of the French examples in the Manuscript, but, once again, the green colour is not a surprise. This uniform in general corresponds closely to the uniform of an Italian Line Fusilier depicted in one of Weiland's plates. The soldier in that print also has a shako, although it has silver chinscales and white cords. As a Fusilier, he naturally also has green shoulder-straps instead of epaulettes and a red collar, piped white (like the Grenadier in the preceding Plate). Two points that are less easy to explain in the Weiland source are the green cuff flaps with four buttons and an infantry sabre and cross-belt for a centre company soldier.

Officier et Voltigeur du prémier Régiment italien

93
Chasseur and Grenadier [Carabinier] of the 1st Regiment of Italian Chasseurs [Light Infantry]

A. Chasseur. The uniform of this figure provides a visual confirmation of the shape and style of dress specified in regulations for Italian light infantry, but a visual contradiction of the accepted view that the colour scheme for those troops did not include the colour red. All sources agree that both Light regiments had yellow vests and lapel trim, so there are no surprises here in that regard, but the red collar and cuffs with yellow trim are not confirmed by any other authority. Moreover, the style of the cuff is more appropriate for a line infantryman. One can only surmise that these new details were adopted by the 1st Regiment during its long sojourn in France as a further means of distinguishing the unit's dress. The massive red and green drooping plume is quite extraordinary, but a more unexpected point about the shako is the fact that the plate, which has a traditional light infantry design incorporating a hunting horn, is of yellow instead of silver metal. The mixed red and green colour of the cords seems right for a Chasseur, but the arrangement of the cords is unusual, the lower cord being significantly thinner than the higher one and they are both draped asymmetrically across the front of the shako.

B. Carabinier. With this painting, one can see that the traditional means of distinguishing the Carabiniers (mis-labelled here as a 'Grenadier') of a light infantry regiment have been fully utilized, with solid red replacing the mixed red and green of the Chasseur in many uniform features. The colour red has even been used to replace the yellow of the trim around the top of the figure's short gaiters. The head-dress looks somewhat unusual, but the Otto artist has apparently attempted to represent an extremely tall fur busby. Both soldiers are carrying muskets with three brass barrel fittings, a feature characteristic of the Year IX Model Dragoon musket which was prescribed for (but seldom used by) French Voltigeurs.[1]

---

1 'Instructions sur les armes à feu . . . ', *Journal Militaire* for 1806, Pt. 1, pp. 197–240, at 205–206.

Chasseur   Grenadier

premier regiment des Chasseur italienne

94

Chasseur [Voltigeur] of the 1st Regiment of Italian Chasseurs [Light Infantry] and Grenadier [Carabinier of the 2nd Light]

A. Voltigeur. Since a Chasseur of the 1st Italian Light Infantry Regiment is illustrated in the preceding Plate and we know that yellow was the traditional distinguishing colour for Voltigeurs, it seems only reasonable to conclude that the caption for this painting is incorrect and that this soldier is in fact a Voltigeur. This conclusion is further borne out by both the similarities and differences between his uniform and that of the Chasseur; they are identical in style and differ only in details of colour, the yellow of the Voltigeur being substituted for the red of the Chasseur in the shako plume and cords, epaulettes, sword knot and gaiter tassel. (The yellow colours in this painting seem to have particularly darkened through discoloration.) The collar has also been changed from red to yellow, and this has caused its trim to be changed as well. The pose of this figure also reveals for the first time in this sequence of paintings about the light infantry that the colour of the jacket turnbacks was yellow rather than the white called for by regulations.

B. Carabinier. The caption for this figure has been cropped (as evidenced by the appearance of the solitary letter 'G' to its right) and the word 'Grenadier' has been written in another hand, so we will never know exactly which unit is intended to be represented in this painting. The red epaulettes and red cords have strong Carabinier connotations, and because this soldier appears in the same painting with another figure from the 1st Italian Light Infantry, it seems logical to attribute him to the same regiment. If this were correct, however, this figure would represent the same kind of soldier as the second figure in Plate No. 93.[1] Such a state of affairs would logically suggest that the uniforms should be identical, but one can plainly see that the second differs from the first in having a drooping yellow plume and a yellow collar trimmed with red. One plausible suggestion that has been put forward to explain these differences is that the two battalions of the 1st Light serving in Germany had different uniforms for their respective Carabinier companies, but there are no other known cases of such battalion distinctions in French Napoleonic armies.[2] Another explanation (which this author favours) is that the figure actually represents a Carabinier of the 2nd Light because of the similarities of his uniform with that of the light infantry figure in Plate No. 97.

---

1 The word 'grenadier' in the caption has been written in a different hand from the rest of the title.
2 Perconte, *Infanterie Légère Italienne*, p. 71.

Chasseur   *du premier Regim:*

des Chasſ: italiens

Grenadier

95
Sapper of the First Regiment of
Italian Chasseurs [Light Infantry]

This intriguing painting demonstrates another aspect of the skills of the Otto artist – a talent for portraiture. The brown skin and curly hair of this figure leave no doubt that the artist was depicting a Negro, a race not prominently represented in the armies of the period.[1] The uniform conforms perfectly to the little that is known about Italian Sapper dress: '... when the troops are on campaign, 8 grenadiers [sic] chosen on a rotating basis will be given axes and aprons and will perform the duties of a sapper ...'[2] So, the soldier here is wearing the same uniform as the preceding Carabinier. He has also obviously picked up some other standard Sapper distinctions: crossed-axes badge,

gauntlets and short musket, as well as a black cartridge box worn on a thin black waist belt.[3] His sabre scabbard seems to have a different tip from the ones in the preceding painting of a Carabinier.

1 The French army did have one unit called the Black Pioneers, which had a rank and file composed exclusively of persons of African descent. This unit was subsequently transferred to the service of Joachim Murat when he became the King of Naples, at which point it was re-named as the Royal African Regiment. Pierre Carles, 'Un Régiment Noir Sous le Premier Empire', *Carnet de la Sabretache* (1967), pp. 342–349.
2 Regulation quoted in Perconte, *Infanterie Légère Italienne*, p. 67.
3 A number of secondary sources depict the waist-belt as having been white. It is not clear whether this error stems from these sources copying each other or copying an inaccurate facsimile of the original painting. See, e.g., R. Forthoffer *Fiche Documentaire* No. 252/253: *Italie – L'Infanterie Légère (I) 1801–1808.*

Sappeur du premier regiment des
Chasseur   italienne

96

Drum Major of the First Regiment
of Italian Chasseurs [Light Infantry]

Italian Drum Majors are not supposed to have had 'any distinctive insignia beyond their stripes of rank', but this painting certainly proves that the soldiers of the Kingdom of Italy were also prone to sartorial excesses.[1] The plume is almost breathtakingly absurd with its three levels of green ostrich feathers, accented by the tall red shaft in front. The air of unreality is enhanced by the fact that the base of the plume originates somewhat mysteriously from the front of the busby with no visible mounting. The cords are configured in the same way as those of the Carabinier, but their gold colour (together with that of the epaulettes and the rank stripes) represents another departure from the standard pattern of having metallic lace follow the colour of the regimental buttons. The uniform jacket has only yellow facings and lace, and none of the red features displayed on the other uniforms of the Regiment illustrated in the Manuscript, so in this regard at least this uniform follows the stated colour scheme for the unit. The details have been reversed, however, so the collar and cuffs are green trimmed yellow rather than yellow trimmed green, and the expected green lapels have become entirely yellow. The lace lacks the bluish overtone used elsewhere in the Manuscript to simulate silver, so it may have been intended to be white in colour. The colour of the breeches has also been changed, and from the glimpse of coat tail between the figure's legs, it seems that the tails were longer than those of other figures, but were still yellow. The buttons of the vest are yellow, but the sabre hilt and scabbard are silver. Zimmerman Drawing No. 14 illustrates an 'Italian Drum Major of the 1st Regiment', but since aside from the use of a busby the uniform illustrated does not match this one, it may be that Zimmerman was observing a Drum Major of the 1st Line rather than the 1st Light. The figure drawn by Zimmerman does, however, have pointed lapels, a detail usually associated with light infantry uniforms.

1   Quoted in Perconte, *Infanterie Légère Italienne*, p. 25.

Tambour Major du ⸻ premier régiment des Chasseur ⸻ italiense

97

Chasseur [Voltigeur] of 1st Italian [Line] Regiment; Grenadier of 2nd Regiment of Italian Chasseurs [Light Infantry]

A. Voltigeur. The white lapels of this soldier mark him clearly as a member of a line rather than a light infantry unit, so the 'Chasseur' designation in the caption must be wrong and he must be a Voltigeur. This being the case, one would have expected his uniform to be identical with that of the Voltigeur of the 1st Line illustrated in Plate No. 92 above, but instead one finds both large and small differences between the two. The most obvious point of departure is the bicorne of this soldier, which has a green pom-pom, green tassels in the corners and a striking orange strip of braid holding the cockade in place. In addition, however, the cuffs are different; in this painting they have yellow trim, and the sword knot is yellow. (The epaulette buttons in this painting are yellow instead of silver, but this may be a mistake, as is the omission of buttons entirely from the right cuff flap.) The likeliest explanation for these differences is to be found in the fact that several detachments of the 1st Line travelled from Italy during the course of 1807 to join the original contingent. Given the general evolution of Napoleonic military dress towards the shako and away from the bicorne, this may be one of the original soldiers while that in Plate No. 92 is one of the reinforcements.

B. Carabinier. The caption specifies that this figure is a member of the 2nd Italian Light Infantry Regiment, and the details of his uniform are almost identical with those of the Carabinier figure in Plate No. 94 above. One point is certainly different between the two paintings – in this case there is a yellow crescent above the fringe on the epaulettes. Another point may be different, but cannot be verified – there is only a single cord across the back of this busby, which may mean that there was only a single cord across the front as well, which would be different from the preceding painting. These differences may be distinctions between the two battalions of the 2nd Light, or between different detachments uniformed at different times from different sources. The rest of the details from this rear view are probably also correct for the uniform of the Carabinier of the 1st Light Regiment, because the two units were supposed to have the same dress. The red grenades in the short turnbacks are a traditional distinction for Carabiniers, but the bright blue greatcoat is not. The fatigue duty cap rolled under the cartridge box seems to be grey with yellow piping and a red tassel. The piping in the coat tails has the normal outline for a vertical pocket except that it takes a chevron form on the upper edge. There also appear to be two silver buttons in the small of the figure's back (the right-hand one of which is more visible), each of which is decorated with four loops of lace.

Chaseur du premier
regiment italienne

Grenadier du second regiment des
Chasseurs   italienne

98

Italian Artilleryman [Sapper];
Grenadier [Carabinier] of the Third [Second]
Regiment of Italian Chasseurs [Light Infantry]

A. Sapper. The uniform of this mysterious figure has a colour scheme that is not consistent with that of any other known Italian uniform of the Napoleonic period. He is certainly not an artilleryman, since Italian artillery uniforms were distinguished with black facings. He may, however, be a member of either Company No. 4 or Company No. 6 in one of the two Sapper Battalions organized in the Italian Army in 1802.[1] (Both those companies were present with the Italian corps in North Germany.) Those soldiers did wear bicornes, green collars, vests and trousers and red jacket lapels. Unfortunately, they were also supposed to have yellow epaulettes, white metal buttons, black piping around the lapels and black cuffs, none of which features can be found in this painting.

B. Carabinier. The caption assigns this figure to the 3rd Italian Light, but although a third light infantry regiment was in fact raised for the Italian Army in July 1807, it apparently never left Italian soil that year. On the other hand, the 2nd Light Regiment is known to have begun experimenting with bright blue facings in 1806, and was actually assigned sky-blue facings when the light infantry uniform regulations were revised on 1 July 1807.[2] It

therefore seems more likely that this figure represents one of the reinforcements for the 2nd Light sent out from the depot in Italy in the course of 1807. This possibility is supported by the fact that the Pegau Chronicle, a chronological listing and description of all troops passing through the German city of Pegau during this era, reports the passage on 21 June 1807 of 400 soldiers of the 1st and 2nd Italian Chasseurs (sic), some of whom 'were dressed in green with blue cuffs'.[3] The shape of the bearskin cap is similar to that of the French Grenadiers and Carabiniers, but different from that of the massive fur busbies worn by the other Italian élite company figures in the Manuscript. The white cords are also surprising given that red cords have been used for all other Italian Carabiniers. There is no mention in other sources of the use of red piping for the collar and cuffs.

---

1 J.-P. Perconte 'Napoleons Alliierte... das königlich italienische Sappeurbataillon 1806–1807', *Die Depesche* No. 4, pp. 11–19. *Die Depesche* is an excellent German-language journal devoted to Napoleonic military history, with a particular emphasis on military uniforms.
2 Perconte, *Infanterie Légère Italienne*, pp. 46–47 and 84.
3 The Pegau Chronicle is set forth in a series of articles entitled 'Die Stadt Pegau zur Franzosenzeit' in R. Knötel, *Mitteilungen zur Geschichte der Militarischen Tracht* for 1904.

Artillerie italienne

Grenadier du troisième
regiment
des Chasseur italienne

APPENDIXES

APPENDIX A
LIST OF UNITS APPEARING
IN THE OTTO MANUSCRIPT

The Imperial Guard

Infantry

Foot Grenadiers

Foot Chasseurs

Fusiliers

Sailors

Cavalry

Mounted Grenadiers

Mounted Chasseurs

Mamelukes

Dragoons

Horse Artillery

Gendarme Orderlies

Guides of Berthier

Line Infantry

3rd Line

8th Line

21st Line

22nd Line

24th Line

25th Line

45th Line

46th Line

54th Line

63rd Line

75th Line

85th Line

94th Line

95th Line

96th Line

Light Infantry and Auxiliaries

9th Light

10th Light

16th Light

1st Paris Guard

2nd Paris Guard

Line Cavalry

Carabiniers

9th Cuirassiers

3rd Dragoons

6th(?) Dragoons

11th(?) Dragoons

20th(?) Dragoons

2nd Hussars

5th Hussars

7th(?) Hussars

5th Chasseurs

24th Chasseurs

26th Chasseurs

Support Units

Horse Artillery

Sappers

Artillery Train

Gendarmes

Italian Units

1st Line

1st Light

2nd Light

Sappers(?)

Source: L. Bennigsen, *Mémoires du Général Bennigsen*, (3 vols., Paris 1907), Annex 28

APPENDIX B
ORGANIZATION OF THE *GRAND ARMEE* 1 JUNE 1807

Units represented in the Otto Manuscript are shown in bold italic.

Imperial Guard – Marshal Bessières
Infantry – General Hulin: ***Grenadiers, Chasseurs, 1st and 2nd Fusiliers*** and ***Seamen***
Cavalry – General Walther: ***Mounted Grenadiers, Mounted Chasseurs, Mamelukes, Dragoons, Gendarme Orderlies*** and ***Horse Artillery***

I Corps – Marshal Bernadotte
Division – General Dupont: ***9th Light***, ***24th***, 32nd and ***96th Line***
Division – General Lapisse: ***16th Light***, ***8th***, ***45th*** and ***54th Line***
Division – General Vilatte: 27th Light, ***63rd***, ***94th*** and ***95th Line***
Light Cavalry – General Beaumont: ***2nd*** and 4th Hussars, ***5th Chasseurs***
Dragoon Division – General La Houssaye: 17th, 18th, 19th and 27th Dragoons

III Corps – Marshal Davout
Division – General Morand: 13th Light, 17th, 30th, 51st, 61st and 65th Line
Division – General Friant: 15th Light, 33rd, 48th, 108th and 111th Line
Division – General Gudin: 7th Light, 12th, ***21st***, ***25th*** and ***85th Line***
Light Cavalry – General Marulaz: 1st, 2nd and 12th Chasseurs

IV Corps – Marshal Soult
Division – General Saint-Hilaire: ***10th Light***, 14th, ***22nd***, 36th, 43rd and 55th Line
Division – General Carra Saint-Cyr: 24th Light, 4th, 28th, ***46th*** and 57th Line
Division – General Legrand: 26th Light, 18th, ***75th*** and 105th Line, Corsican and Po Sharpshooters
Light Cavalry – General Guyot: 8th Hussars, 16th and ***26th Chasseurs***

V Corps – Marshal Massena
Division – General Suchet: 17th Light, 34th, 40th, 64th and 88th Line
Division – General Gazan: 21st and 28th Light, 100th and 103rd Line
Division – General Wrede: Bavarians
Light Cavalry – General Montbrun: 10th Hussars, 21st Chasseurs
Dragoon Division – General Lorge: 13th, 15th, 22nd and 25th Dragoons

VI Corps – Marshal Ney
Division – General Marchand: 6th and 31st Light, 39th, 69th and 76th Line
Division – General Bisson: 25th Light, 27th, 50th and 59th Line
Light Cavalry – General Colbert: 3rd Hussars, 10th and 15th Chasseurs

VIII Corps – Marshal Mortier
Division – General Dupas: 4th Light, 15th and 58th Line, ***Paris Guard*** and Wurzburg Regiment

Division – General Loison: *1st* and *2nd Italian Light*, *1st Italian Line*, Poles, Saxons and Württembergers

Division – General Dombrowski: 2 Polish infantry regiments, 2 Polish cavalry regiments

Division – General Zajoncek: 2 Polish infantry regiments, 2 Polish cavalry regiments

Cavalry – General Dury: 2nd Dutch Cuirassiers, 2nd Dutch Hussars

Reserve Corps – Marshal Lannes

Division – General Oudinot: 8 élite regiments

Division – General Verdier: 2nd and 12th Light, *3rd* and 72nd Line

Division – General Von Polenz: Saxons

Cavalry – General Von Besser: 9th Hussars, Saxons

Reserve Cavalry – Marshal Murat

Light Cavalry Division – General Lasalle: 1st, *5th* and *7th Hussars*, 3rd, 7th, 11th, 13th, 20th, 22nd and *24th Chasseurs*, Bavarian and Württemberg Light Horse

Heavy Cavalry Division – General Nansouty: 1st and 2nd *Carabiniers*, 2nd, 3rd, *9th* and 12th Cuirassiers

Heavy Cavalry Division – General Saint-Sulpice: 1st, 5th, 10th and 11th Cuirassiers

Heavy Cavalry Division – General Espagne: 4th, 6th, 7th and 8th Cuirassiers

Dragoon Division – General Latour-Maubourg: 1st, 2nd, 4th, 14th, *20th*(?) and 26th Dragoons

Dragoon Division – General Klein: *3rd*, *6th*(?), 10th and *11th*(?) *Dragoons*

Dragoon Division – General Milhaud: 5th, 8th, 9th, 12th, 16th and 21st Dragoons